KILLER CAMELS FROM KUWAIT:

The Saudi Stories

By

Christopher Larsen

ISBN: 0-75963-758-X

This book is printed on acid free paper.

1stBooks - rev. 06/06/01

TABLE OF CONTENTS

An Angry Camel

Hobbled Camel

KILLER CAMELS FROM KUWAIT

The bull camel spit on the back of the Bedouin's head. It was the second time in two days. The first time was when the Bedouin hobbled him to keep him from wondering off. This time, the Bedouin had just finished removing a sharp stone from the camel's right front foot.

When it first happened, the Bedouin sympathized with the hobbled camel and let it pass. This time, though, he felt the camel's ingratitude. He did not bother to wipe the putrid dark slime from his gutra. The metal pry bar used to remove the stone became a convenient weapon. He spun around with all his strength and slammed the metal bar broadside against the camel's jaw. The camel bawled loudly and jumped back a few steps. The next several seconds was a stare-down between the beast and the man. The camel yielded and slowly walked away toward the rest of the herd.

That night, as the Bedouin lay sleeping under the stars on a thin, vinyl-covered foam pad, the injured camel snuck over to him and stepped squarely on his stomach. He then proceeded to bite the Bedouin's arms, neck and face. The Bedouin made one loud shout and then was quiet. The camel stood with his foot on the man's stomach. He put his nose close to the Bedouin's bloody face. It appeared he was making sure the man was dead.

The one witness to the event was the man's terrified eleven-year-old son. He was sleeping in the back of their Toyota pickup and awoke when the camel stepped on his father. The policeman who investigated allowed the son to use an assault rifle from the patrol vehicle to put down the camel. A Kuwaiti friend who knew one of the investigating policemen told me the details of this incident. There was a brief summary of the incident in the Kuwaiti English-language newspaper in 1986; I don't remember which month.

A few months after the Kuwait incident, two Yemeni truck drivers were camping in the Saudi desert south of the Kuwaiti

1

border. They were making a run from Amman, Jordan to Jeddah, Saudi Arabia. Several Camels were grazing nearby. The two managed to get a rope around one cow. They tied her to the back of their truck while they dug a shallow pit. They then led the camel into the pit and buried her lower legs in the sand. Once the camel was immobilized, one of the Yemenis sexually assaulted the camel.

Fearing the wrath of the camel's owner, should they be discovered, the two men began digging the sand away from the camel's legs. After they had removed some of the sand, the annoyed camel managed to pull free and began chasing and biting them. The man who had not assaulted the camel jumped onto the side of the large stake-bed truck and climbed to safety. The other man had opened the door to the cab of the truck and was trying to climb in when the outraged camel spun around and kicked the door with both back feet. The man's head was crushed between the edge of the door and the door jam.

The camel only kicked once, but it was enough to kill her assailant. The man who had not assaulted the camel told the police and the camel's owner what had happened. The story did not make the paper or the evening news. Word of mouth spread the story throughout Kuwait and Saudi Arabia. The man who told me about this did not know what happened to the survivor. A normal punishment for such a crime is 40 lashes and some jail time. In some areas, though, a beheading may be required.

From conversations with a Kuwaiti camel owner, I learned several important things about camels: Camels have distinct personalities, are highly intelligent and have long memories. You should never be mean to a camel; they will remember, and they will get you. Some camels are just mean by nature and some are quite gentle. Camels respond to firm commands but prefer to be sweet-talked (in Arabic). Never ever turn your back on a camel you don't know. Camels can and do kill.

Camels attack and kill a few people every year in the Middle East. These direct attacks, though, only account for a few of the camel-related deaths. The real camel-danger is on the highway.

There are no fences, and the whole country is an open range. Camels amble wherever they wish. Quite often, they wish to amble down the highway. Adult camels weigh in at well over one ton.

There are no enforced speed limits in the Middle East. People drive at night at speeds over 100 MPH. Several people each month discover that camels come out at night and hang out just around the bend or just over the top of the hill. Foxes and sheep also hang out in these same areas—but foxes and sheep don't weigh 2,500 pounds.

An English friend was in a hurry to get to the airport one night. He was on his way to pickup his wife whom he had not seen in nearly four months. I heard that he crested a hill on the freeway and sheered the legs out from under a large bull camel. The camel's body took off the top of the car along with the top of my friend. The camel's owner wanted the widow to pay for the dead animal. I believe she was able to return to London before it became an issue.

My own run-in with a camel happened on the road between Jeddah and Yanbu, the same road where my friend died. It happened long before my friend's accident and long before I talked to that camel-owner in Kuwait. I spotted a large herd of camels just off the road and drove my truck into the herd. A few camels moved out of my way; the rest ignored me. I got out of my truck and began photographing camels with my zoom lens. The cows didn't mind; the bull did.

I walked right up to the bull. He looked at me briefly and then put his head down to graze. I pointed my zoom lens at his head and tried to focus on his eye. When his head disappeared from the viewfinder, I lowered the camera to see what was going on. To my horror, he was lunging at my face with his mouth wide open. I spun and ran. I heard his jaw chomp just behind my head and felt his breath on my neck. Pure adrenaline allowed me to jump onto the hood of my truck and then spring up onto the roof. When I stood up, the camel stopped. We just stared at each other.

Several minutes passed before a Mercedes dump truck stopped alongside the road about 150 feet from my truck. The passenger-side door opened. The man inside was laughing quite loudly. For a while he just laughed. Then, he got out and walked over to the camel.

It was amazing how he was able to sweet-talk that bull. The camel just turned and walked back into the herd. Still laughing, the old Bedouin helped me down and lectured me in a language I did not understand. I thanked him profusely in a language he did not understand, but we communicated. He was still chuckling as he returned to his truck.

After that close encounter of a camel kind, I bought a 500 mm lens with a doubler and took all my camel photographs from inside vehicles or from other safe locations. That experience put too much fear in me to try riding one. It did, however, make it that much easier to eat one—part of one, anyway. If you ever have the opportunity to eat camel meat, don't pass it up. It is a lean red meat with a mellow taste similar to elk. It is neither gamy nor tough.

If you are driving in the Middle East, beware: Camels are a serious road hazard and you are libel to the camel's owner if you hit one. If you do not survive, your spouse could be libel.

If you want to ride a camel, there is always a Bedouin willing to let you ride for a fee. Riding on that swaying hump is said to be quite a thrill. Riding them any other way, though, can get you killed.

Killer Camels From Kuwait

A Village Built Around an Old Turkish Fort in Katif

Local Boy Cleaning His Goats in The Outflow From The Local Artesian Well

SLAVERY AND CONTRACT LABOR

Simon was delivered with a warning that he was lazy and needed a good whipping now and then. He was tall, rather scrawny and had facial scars. Other than the scars, he looked and smelled O.K. It really didn't matter; my boss could not refuse the gift. He thanked the man and took Simon inside.

Simon's former owner considered him a troublesome slave. He was given as a bonus for some work done on a palace garden. The project had a few problems, so a less-than-perfect gift was considered appropriate. Had the project gone smoother, the gift might have been an attractive female. Had the project been more flawed, the gift might have only appeared to be an attractive female.

My boss had no idea what to do with Simon. He could not turn him out onto the street because he was now my boss's property. He could not send him back to Africa because Simon was born into slavery in Saudi Arabia. After a few days of pondering the situation, my boss made Simon his personal driver. He let Simon live in a spare bedroom. He treated him as part of the family. He was paid a regular salary, ate with my boss's family, and was included in many of their family activities. Simon had a relatively good life—but he was still a slave.

Before I had a Saudi driver license, Simon drove me wherever I needed to go. He was a whiner, but I enjoyed his stories. He was preoccupied with saving up enough money to leave Saudi Arabia and with becoming a free man. He asked a lot about America, but for economic reasons, was more interested in Europe. Over the five-year period that I knew him, he eventually focused on Italy. The last time I saw Simon, he was grinning like the Cheshire cat. He was on his way to the airport to catch a plane to Rome. It was a one-way ticket.

Simon was an exception. Most slaves where freed in the early 1960's when slavery in Saudi Arabia was abolished. That ban, however, did not automatically free every slave. Many slaves were illiterate and could not understand their new options. Some slaves were never given options. For one reason or another, many just stayed where they were and let life go on. Their real gain was that they no longer had to worry about their families being split-up at the auction block.

A friend who remodeled a palace for a prince told me that a eunuch guarded the woman's quarters (harem). The eunuch was a very large black man with no tongue and no testicles. My friend told me that the guard became a eunuch as a young boy when it was common for rich men to have eunuch slaves guard their women.

In fairness to the Saudi government, the current situation is not one of forced labor with overseers and whips. Of all those in slavery prior to the early 1960's, most were given full citizenship, and many where given free education and interest-free government loans to start a business. Some are now successful businessmen, and some are now surviving as day laborers or beggars.

A few Saudis have family servants that more or less belong to them. Their ex-slaves have no real choice but to live in servitude. Some of these servants are treated worse than before they were freed. In most cases, though, the family servants are considered as, and treated as, extended family members. It is not uncommon for the female children of former slaves to marry the male children of former masters. Most of these ex-slaves live a much better life than they would if they were forced to leave. For those who want to leave, though, it can be brutal.

An American Friend living in Riyadh was driving to an agricultural area called Al Karj. While driving his car on a rural road, he was quickly passed by a pickup and a Mercedes. It was obvious that one was chasing the other. About 500 yards in front of him, the Mercedes ran the pickup off the road. As he approached, he saw the man in the truck jump out and run. Two men from the Mercedes jumped out and chased him. My friend slowed down to see what was happening. He saw two Saudis chase down a black man. The two Saudis caught the man and knocked him to the ground. When my friend was nearly to the point where the vehicles had left the road, he saw one Saudi hold the man down while the other Saudi smashed the man's skull with a large rock. As my friend drove by, the two Saudis were walking back to their Mercedes. He drove by without altering his speed or turning his head. Then, to his relief, the Saudis got into their car and drove off in the opposite direction. There was no mention of the incident in the local paper or on the local news.

When we were in school, we learned that Abraham Lincoln freed the slaves. I thought that meant all slaves. We weren't taught that the economy of Saudi Arabia was based on slavery. We were told only of human rights violations in the USSR and in China. I suspect the reality of Arab slavery was hidden from us because of our dependence on Saudi oil. As we have become dependent on their oil, however, they have become dependent on our money. That's probably the real reason the Saudis banned slavery. A royal decree was issued, and that potential roadblock to international business was quietly removed. It was never front-page news.

That political slight-of-hand worked in Washington and in other capitals, but it created a serious problem for Saudi society. One day, slaves did all the manual labor. The next day, all the slaves became employees. What was a good Bedouin to do? The Saudi Government decided that slave labor could be replaced with contract labor. There would be no more slavery, just free men working for wages for a set contract period. The concept pleased the international community. No politician would have to explain why his or her country supported a government that embraced slavery.

On the surface, the concept of contract labor sounds like a normal job. Labor unions sign labor contracts for their members so they can have a good job and good benefits. The concept of contract labor was sold as something similar. In reality, it is just a modified version of traditional slavery.

What was once a slavery network is now a labor-recruiting network. Labor recruiters in many third-world countries advertise good-paying jobs in Saudi Arabia. Both the Saudi employers and the recruits pay a fee to the employment agency. For the recruiters, the new arrangement is better than slavery because the resource now comes to them, and they extract money from both ends. In essence, a slaver by any other name makes more money.

How this works for the average laborer is tragic. A man, let's call him Fernando, cannot find work for more than a few dollars per day in his country even though he has an engineering degree. He visits a labor recruiter in Manila. His sister Yolanda, who has just graduated from nursing school, goes with him. They are told there are many common-labor jobs available. They are told that for an extra fee they can get better positions that are in line with their qualifications. They each agree on an upfront fee that is equal to about twenty percent of their expected pay for the two-year contract. Since they do not have the money up front, they must sign a paper giving the labor recruiter a lien on part of their salary. The paper allows the recruiter to collect half of their salary directly from the employer. The agreement states that once the employment fee plus interest is collected, the lien will be removed. With only sketchy information about the actual jobs, they each sign a two-year contract.

They are given tickets and their passports with entry visas. They are told to look for someone at the Saudi airport holding up a sign with the recruiting company's name. They are not told that their new employer, also called a sponsor, will legally confiscate and hold their passports. They are not told that they cannot seek other employment if they are unhappy. They are not told that they will have no rights against their employer but their employer will have absolute control over their lives. They are not told that they cannot leave the country without an exit visa—a document that only their sponsor can obtain. They are not told that nonperformance of their contract duties is a criminal offense. The recruiter's in-kingdom agent collects them from the airport and distributes them to their waiting sponsors.

Fernando finds that he has been hired as a plumber. His pay is as expected: $300 per month of which $150 is automatically sent to the recruiter. He is given a bunk in a rented villa. He shares a large room with 14 other workers. They sleep on triple-decker bunks. He learns that he must buy food from the money he is allowed to keep. By pooling resources, he and several others in the same predicament, manage to keep monthly food costs to $50 per month each. He was counting on sending most of his money to his wife, but finds he can only send $100 per month from his regular pay (about what he made back home). He likes the job. He finds he can earn monthly bonuses by doing an exceptional job. He sends his bonus money to his wife and keeps his spirits up knowing that once the employment fee is paid, his family will do well.

Yolanda finds out she has been hired as a nanny. She is told she will have a room of her own, all food and clothing are furnished, and if they are happy with her, an occasional bonus may be in order. She is told that she may consider herself part of the family. The job conditions sound good, but she feels betrayed by the recruiter who promised her a key nursing position in the new King Khalid hospital. Her feeling of betrayal changes to fear when she is introduced to the children—three teenage boys. She protests that a mistake has been made and is told, "No, you appear to be exactly what the recruiter promised."

The first day, Yolanda tries in vain to assert herself and gain some measure of control over the three youths. That afternoon, she is raped by each of the boys. In tears, she pleads with the mother to put a stop to their actions. She is slapped repeatedly and told that she will only receive a bonus if she keeps the boys happy. She is also informed that she cannot leave the villa except to go shopping with the mother. There are bars on all windows and she is kept locked in her room until her services are needed.

She pretends to enjoy her new job so as to win the confidence of one of the boys. She singles out the youngest one and eventually persuades him to let her go outside for some fresh air. She flags down a car driven by an American man who takes her to her country's embassy. They tell her that there is nothing they can do other than send a written protest to the Saudi government. An embassy driver returns her to the villa.

That night the mother whips her with a fiberglass rod so badly that the father intercedes and takes her to a local clinic for medical care. At the clinic, she pleads with anyone who will listen—begging for help. Everyone at the clinic offers their sympathy and explains that it is too dangerous for them to help. When she is left alone for a few minutes in a treatment room, she finds a single-edge razor blade and fatally slashes her neck. The Saudi sponsor is questioned but not detained. The clinic supervisor is taken to jail. The American who gave her a ride is deported. Yolanda's body is taken to the morgue at the new King Khalid hospital.

Yolanda's story was told to me by one of her brothers who worked for me as a plumber. Although the Yolanda story is an extreme case, hers is but one of several such stories I heard while living in Saudi Arabia. I am telling her story because the anguish on her brother's face deeply moved me. Please understand, though, that most Saudis are horrified by such conduct. This story represents a serious social problem that many Saudis are aware of but are powerless to affect. A few Saudi businessmen are doing what they can to change the laws that allow such things. Such criminal behavior is not an Islamic tradition.

Many labor problems occur because of voids in the labor laws. One such problem happened to a Filipino in Riyadh. His name was Enrico. Two of his relatives worked for me. His relatives relayed his story to me as it unfolded. Enrico worked for a large Saudi construction company. He had been in Saudi for almost five years. His sponsor, whom he had seen only a few times, left the country shortly after signing the biggest contract they had ever procured. No one suspected a problem until the end of the month came and the British project manager showed up ashen-faced. His sponsor, who was due back the day before, had not returned to sign the payroll checks. Enrico was told he would have to wait until the sponsor returned to get paid. After a week passed with no pay, he found out from the project manager that the sponsor had transferred a $20-million advance payment for the project to a Swiss bank account. The sponsor's brother, who was a partner, was desperately trying to find him. The brother arranged for all 165 workers to get half their pay and then he disappeared. The brother left with almost nothing. If the brother had stayed, he would have been jailed when the company defaulted on the contract.

After a month passed, all 165 men were evicted from their three rented villas because their rent was unpaid. Most of them had other relatives working on other projects. They were housed and fed by their cousins, nephews and uncles. Some men found illegal work for cash. Most found that no one was willing to risk jail by hiring them.

Enrico had a brother with a good sponsor who had close ties to the Royals. His brother's boss took him in. He was fed and given money each month even though he could not legally work. Within a month, his brother's sponsor had procured a release from Enrico's previous company and became Enrico's new sponsor. Many of his fellow workers were not as lucky.

Most of the men survived on local handouts and money sent to them by relatives. Their families back home were destitute. Enrico's new sponsor eventually managed to petition the King and get exit visas and tickets home for the other workers. The whole process took over one year. There are no laws to protect laborers from such situations.

There are thousands of Fernandos, Yolandas and Enricos working in Saudi Arabia. These contract laborers provide an internationally acceptable alternative to the old ways. There is no slavery—just free enterprise. And with most embassies sticking their heads in the sand, there are no human rights violations, either.   Human rights violations only happen in countries that don't export oil.

A Really Old Building at Hofuf

Remains of An Old Turkish Outpost Near Jubail

LAW AND ORDER

Someone once said, "The more laws we write, the more criminals we create." If that is true, how can Saudi Arabia, a country where nearly everything is illegal, claim to have almost no crime? They do have the military, the National Guard, the local police, the secret police and the religious police, but how do they do it?

Their military is pretty much like any other military; they defend against foreign invaders. Though many Saudis believe all foreigners are invaders, the military generally does not harass foreign workers.

National Guard troops handle internal security. The head of the National Guard is Crown Price Abdullah (maybe King Abdullah by the time this is published). His troops protect the Royal Family and keep the civil order. The Saudi National Guard has the countries best troops. These soldiers are as good as our special forces at surviving and fighting in the desert— maybe better. Fear of these troops keeps the grumblers from becoming rebels. When a few hardy fools decide to take on the government, these guys deal with it—their way. Enemies not fortunate enough to be slaughtered immediately often take a trip behind the sun: they are abandoned far out in the open desert with no food or water. A few example-setters may be sent to chop-chop square.

Local police seem to have only one function: they put people in jail. People are arrested and jailed for almost any reason; breaking a law is not a prerequisite. Local police will incarcerate a person for anyone of influence who wants to put someone in jail. With the exception of serious criminal cases, getting someone out of jail is usually a matter of money.

The secret police are the CIA of Saudi Arabia. Everyone fears the secret police. They are the check and balance system over the local police. They are the men responsible for taking police that rape and murder to chop-chop square. These

17

dedicated men keep the white-collar criminals, organized criminals and political dissidents constantly looking over their shoulder.

The Mutawwi'un are the religious police. These men have no counterpart in the West. The closest comparison might be the thought police in Orwell's *1984*. These uniformed men cruise the streets with Chevy Suburbans, bullhorns and riding crops. They enforce their version of Islamic law. They use the bullhorns to remind everyone when it is prayer time. They use the riding crops to smack people for minor infractions. They use the Suburbans to haul people to jail for not following or respecting Islamic law. The Mutawwi'un are the enforcers of the state religion. They are involved with most of the executions and dismemberments. Even the Royals fear them.

For expatriates, though, the local police are the boogiemen. Most encounters with the local police are related to driving a vehicle or being in the wrong place at the wrong time. However, any of the following reasons may land you in the Calaboose:

- ☹ Fighting
- ☹ Arguing
- ☹ Accidentally entering a harem
- ☹ Staring at or trying to talk to a Saudi woman
- ☹ Drinking, selling or possessing alcohol
- ☹ Parking in the wrong place
- ☹ Not having all the correct papers at a check point
- ☹ Being a project manager when anyone working under you breaks a law
- ☹ Being a project manager when anyone working under you damages someone else's property
- ☹ Looking guilty near a crime scene
- ☹ Being stupid enough to hang around at an accident scene
- ☹ Reporting a crime (you are automatically a suspect)
- ☹ Possession of pornography (a Jane Fonda workout video qualifies)

☹ Being in possession of anything that the police might consider contraband (in one case, a laser printer qualified because the police thought the laser might be uses as a weapon)

☹ Not being conservatively dressed

☹ Cross dressing

☹ Throwing a newspaper in the trash (if it is a local paper with a passage from the Koran printed on any page)

☹ Giving the "Peace" sign.

Each of the above actually caused someone I knew of to have an encounter with the local police. Here are a few of those stories:

The American Muslim: A Lebanese-American friend made his first pilgrimage to Mecca. He was quite euphoric about being in a city where non-Muslims are forbidden. In his giddiness, he flashed the peach sign at the first Mutawwi'un he saw. He was promptly arrested. After a few hours of grilling and admonishing, he was released.

It all turned out to be just a misunderstanding. My friend had not realized that it was a local custom in Mecca to hold up one finger to signify one God. When the Mutawwi'un saw him hold up two fingers, it was taken as a statement that there are two Gods. If things had gone poorly for my friend, I wouldn't have this story to tell. Whenever I see him now, I hold up one finger. He doesn't laugh.

The Architect: A Lebanese architect in Jeddah designed a twenty-six-story office building for a local Saudi businessman. The businessman got together with the building contractor and decided to add six more floors to the building. They also saved some money by using undersized re-bar and substandard concrete. The architect had nothing to do with those behind-the-scene dealings. However, he was on the scene when the building collapsed and killed thirty workers.

The police took him directly from the site to jail. Within a very short time, they transferred him to a local prison. I never heard anything about charges or a trial. I only heard that he was in prison and would have to stay there until things quieted down. It was also mentioned that blood money would have to be paid to all the families with relatives killed when the building collapsed.

Fortunately for the Lebanese architect, he had friends and family with money and influence. After a few years, when things quieted down, families were paid off and he was released. Of course, being Lebanese, just before being released from prison he negotiated a contract with the Saudi government to design a new prison.

The Egyptian: Shukri, an Egyptian truck driver, was quick tempered, arrogant and obnoxious—and he was a good driver. We put up with his demeanor because good drivers were hard to find. One evening, Shukri met a local Saudi neighbor who was not so motivated to overlook his bad manors.

Shukri had driven several workers to their shared villa in downtown Yanbu Al Bar. He parked his truck in the shade beside the villa. As he got out, a Saudi neighbor told him to move his truck because that was the Saudi's normal parking place. Shukri made a comment about the man's mother and walked into the villa.

Several minutes later, the local police arrested Shukri. The police did not have or need a warrant. The police did not tell anyone why they were taking him or where they were taking him. It took several phone-calls the next morning to discover which neighborhood jail had him.

Once we knew where Shukri was, one of our Lebanese engineers started a daily routine of taking food and water to him. We had to provide his daily rations because jail guards provide only bread and water. The bread may be moldy and the water may or may not be fit to drink. I remember thinking that Shukri's dependence on our help would somehow improve his personality.

The same engineer that located Shukri and kept him fed also negotiated his release. The whole process took about a month. After many calls and personal trips to the jail, our engineer finally had everyone in agreement about releasing Shukri. As an educational experience, he invited me to go with him for the final negotiations.

The jail looked about like you'd expect any jail to look. It was dirty, dark, had bars, and was filled with lots of unhappy people. There was upwards of twenty men crammed into one cell the size of a small bedroom. There was a single incandescent bulb hanging from the ceiling in the center of the room. There were no beds. The concrete floor was sloped to the back. Across the back of the room was a shallow trench that extended through a small hole in each wall. Several times a day, water was hosed down the trench. I was told you get used to the stench. Knowing Shukri had survived a month here gave me a new respect for the man.

We passed by the cell area and went upstairs to the captain's office. It was a large room with a huge desk and some tasteless furniture placed there to impress. As the engineer had tea with the captain and did the final negotiations for Shukri's release, my eyes focused on the once-beautiful handmade carpet directly in front of the captain's desk. The entire center was matted with a thick layer of old blood. There appeared to be several different blood-trails on the floor. All of those trails followed the same general route from the office door to a position directly in front of the captain's desk. It was the kind of thing you couldn't help noticing. It was also the kind of thing you did not question.

The conversation between our engineer and the captain went from being falsely friendly to being genuinely angry. An agreement was reached. Money was paid. A release slip was issued—then our engineer started shouting. A guard left the room and returned with some information for the captain. Our engineer and the captain were shouting at the guard. A receipt was issued and we took Shukri back to his villa. His personality had improved.

On the way back to our office, our engineer explained that the Captain had wanted 600 Riyals. Our engineer was offering 100 Riyals (about $30). They agreed on 300 Riyals. When he asked for a receipt, the Captain asked him if he knew why Shukri was there. He said he did not and asked the Captain to please explain. The Captain had asked because he didn't know. A guard was sent to ask other officials in the jail. It turned out that no one knew why Shukri was there. The captain gave us a receipt that said Shukri had done some obscure traffic violation. We wondered how long they would have kept Shukri there if we had not interceded. We also wondered how many people had found themselves in Shukri's predicament, and with no friends, languished in jail until they starved to death or died from some common infection.

Shukri quit his job and returned to Egypt shortly after being released from the Yanbu jail.

The Arizonan: A Saudi in Dhahran ran a red light and smashed into my friend's car. My friend went to jail. The logic was simple. If he had not been in Saudi Arabia just then, the Saudi would not have crashed. Therefore, it was his fault. End of story. Fortunately for my friend, he was working for ARAMCO. The ARAMCO legal department had him out of jail the next day, but that was one day too many. He quit that week and went back to Arizona.

Shah: An Indian man working at our Riyadh office was arrested for a minor traffic infraction. It took over a week of phone calls to find out where Shah was being held. Each time we located him, they transferred him to another jail. It then took another week to find him again. That cat-and-mouse game continued until Shah had been transferred to nearly every jail in Riyadh. With a great deal of persistence, our office manager was able to free Shah after two months. Neither Shah nor our office manager had any idea why the Riyadh police chose to play such a game. One of our Lebanese plumbers had this to offer: "The police in this country are only here to cause trouble. Don't ask why they do what they do. Just run away whenever you see them."

The Syrian: Majhid made me laugh. I remember that he could not pronounce the letter "P." Pepsi Cola was Bebsi Cola and project manager was bro-ject manager. He had an interesting outlook on everything. He once told me that he didn't understand why Americans were enemies with the Soviets. "You are both alike, you know," he told me. "You are both rude, pushy, arrogant and don't respect our religion. The only difference I can see is Americans have more money." His comment wasn't meant as an insult; it was just an honest observation.

One day Majhid came into the office visibly shaken and angry. He had just come from the police station. He had been a passenger in a car driven by his uncle. A Yemeni taxi driver had run a red light and hit their car on the driver's side. His uncle was badly hurt and was bleeding profusely. The police and a Green Crescent ambulance arrived at the scene at almost the same time. The police lieutenant in charge made everyone fill out a report before he would let the ambulance attendants treat the injured. The ambulance guys and Majhid were pleading with the officer to at least let his uncle be taken to the hospital. Their pleadings were rebuked with loud shouts and threats that everyone would go to jail if they wouldn't be still. By the time all the reports were finished, Majhid's uncle had bled to death. Majhid's experience shed light on the bloody carpet in the police captain's office.

The Neighbor: One of my neighbors in Yanbu was arrested at one of the many highway checkpoints. His crime was not having a current company permission document to be on that particular road at that particular time. He had such a permission slip, but it had expired three days earlier. He went to jail. Knowing my neighbor, he probably gave the police a verbal thrashing while he was their guest. His company had him out within twenty-four hours.

23

Two days after he returned home, the police came back. They pushed their way in, searched the house and took several boxes of things with them. A short while later, they returned again and arrested him. I heard that he had been charged with possession of pornography and that the evidence was a Jane Fonda workout tape. I never saw him again.

Five Young Saudis: Five Saudi teens were arrested for deviant sexual behavior. They were convicted of wearing women's clothing and of performing deviant sexual acts with each other. They were all convicted and given between 5 and 7 years in prison. In addition to prison time, they were ordered to receive over 2,000 lashes each. The lashings were to be given fifty at a time with a two-week rest period between sessions. I suspect the Mutawwi'un responsible for bringing those criminals to justice placed bets on how many sessions each could take before dying from an infected wound.

The Armenian: An Armenian friend managed a nursery in Riyadh. A Bedouin truck driver wanted him to sign for a load of substandard plants. When he refused, the driver left. The driver returned a little while later with the police and with two Egyptian laborers. The two laborers were brought along as witnesses to my friend's crime. The driver had told the police that my friend had cursed God. The two laborers, who were not present when the driver first came, swore that he most certainly had cursed God.

My friend's boss came by the site just as the police were taking my friend away in handcuffs. His boss persuaded the police to let him go if he apologized to the driver and promised never to curse God again. Considering the alternative, he apologized—but he still wouldn't accept the substandard plants.

Me: I was never jailed, but I had some close calls. One mishap occurred when I parked in an unmarked no-parking zone. My car was towed to an impound lot. It was easy to find the right police station. It was just around the corner. It was simply a matter of paying a $100 fine and getting a release paper for my car. Well, it was simple up to that point, anyway.

When I tried to drive my car out of the impound lot, I quickly realized why there was no fence or guard. The entire lot was a giant sand box with soft blow-sand several feet deep. Once I had my car buried up to the doors, a smiling old man came over and offered to get me out with his balloon-tired 4x4. For another $100, I was on my way home. I suspect the old man's son was the local police captain.

An opportunity to visit another police station came when one of our trucks ended up in their impound lot. It was at the same jail where Shukri had stayed, so I knew right where to go. I took the same engineer along to translate and do all the negotiating. He had already finished the preliminary over-the-phone work, so we did not anticipate any problems getting our truck back. It was a Toyota 4 x 4 so we figured the soft sand wouldn't be a problem.

We negotiated, paid the fine and received a receipt. We went back downstairs to get the key from the Saudi at the main entrance. We showed our receipt and requested the key. He opened a large drawer and pointed. There were at least five hundred loose keys in that drawer; there were less than fifty cars in the lot. As the old Saudi watched, we went through the mass of keys selecting only the new Toyota keys. After about 20 minutes, we had a pile of thirty or so keys. I went to pick up the pile, and the man grabbed my hand.

"La La La, Wha-hed," he shouted angrily at me. He was saying "No no no, one."

We took one key. As we were going out the door, he pushed the keys we had just sorted back into the drawer and mixed them up with his hands. We spent two hours going back and forth with one key at a time. Each time we went for another key, he would put the one we had just tried back into the pile and mix them up again. I don't know how many times we tried the same key. It became evident that we couldn't win his game. We ended up having a locksmith come out to make a new key. There was a strong family resemblance between the Saudi Key man and the locksmith.

Over a nine-year period, I had many other minor brushes with the local police and the Mutawwi'un. I learned where not to be—and when not to be there. After awhile, the constant threat to my freedom became background stress. It became a lot easier for me once I understood the difference between American police and Saudi police: The Saudi police were not there to protect my freedom—they were there to limit it.

Potter's Cave at the Edge of the Hofuf Oasis

Modern Bedouin Encampment

HOLY MEN

Five times each day, loud speakers in every neighborhood in Saudi Arabia blare out the call to prayer. The faithful and the not so faithful wash, spread their rugs and bow down. Merchants hurry people outside and lock the doors. To ignore prayer time is to invite trouble from the Mutawwi'un.

Prayer call came once while I was standing in the checkout line with a cart full of ice cream. I had to leave it. When prayer time was over, and I was allowed back inside, the ice cream was dripping onto the floor below the grocery cart. I put the ice cream back. God was obviously answering my prayer about staying on my diet.

The annoying thing about prayer time is that it is not optional. A Mutawwi'un in Riyadh whacked a Christian Lebanese friend on the legs until he finally bowed down and prayed. He tried to explain to them in Arabic that he was a Christian. Their logic was simple: looks like a Muslim, sounds like a Muslim, prays like a Muslim.

One day, while observing the Mutawwi'un ride herd over the faithful, my thoughts ran back to what Sister Mary What's-her-name told me in second grade. She told the whole class that all Muslims and Jews were enemies of God. She emphasized that it was the Jews who killed Jesus. Somehow, she managed to lump Jews and Muslims into the same undesirable package. It wasn't until fourth grade that I learned that Jesus was a Jew and that Sister Mary What's-her-name was wrong about a lot of things.

My first observation of Islam was that it was as oppressive as Sister Mary What's-her-name. To me, Mutawwi'un were just paramilitary nuns. I was in Saudi about a year before meeting an old man who showed me a different view of Islam.

While working at the ARAMCO Ras Tanura facility, I met an old Saudi Imam named Abdul Wahed. An Imam is kind of like a priest or minister. They provide the voice you hear on the loud speaker at prayer time. This particular old man provided some services to ARAMCO. I don't remember exactly what he was doing at Ras Tanura. What I do remember is that the old man had charisma. One look at his clear dark eyes and gentle Buddha-like smile and you instantly liked him. I may not have understood everything he said, but I listened. I found myself thinking, "Why aren't there more people like this in the world."

One Friday, shortly after Mosque, I saw Abdul walking near the ARAMCO family housing area. I am not sure what it was, but he seemed to be glowing. He was a striking figure with a majestic white beard and immaculate white thobe. I caught up with him and walked beside him. As we talked, he held my hand. (Men holding hands is a cultural thing in Saudi Arabia. It is not an indication of sexual preference.) He talked of spiritual things with the conviction of someone who knows. I listened intently to the truth of an old grandfather.

I don't remember everything he said, but I do remember what it was like to walk beside the man. The man knew God. You could see God's love in Abdul, and when walking beside him and holding his hand, you could feel a warm energy that was like a gentle electric current. For me, Abdul was one of God's messengers letting me know that God loves everyone—even if they aren't Catholic.

I do not know how many Abdul Waheds there are in the Middle East. I hope there are many. Over a nine-year period, I came to believe that the Muslims pray to the same God I pray to and that for them, Mohammed was a prophet of God. Although I remain firm in my Christian beliefs, I do admire and respect the many faithful who truly follow that path. True followers of Islam don't do the horrible deeds described in this book. My prayer is that all Muslims be as filled with God's love as my friend Abdul.

Islam—Abdul Wahed's Islam—is good. How man has used Islam to make the Middle East the paradise it is today is interesting. A friend who had worked in both Saudi Arabia and Russia told me he felt freer and less oppressed in the Soviet Union than he did in Saudi Arabia. "At least in Russia," he said,

"they don't cut your head off for looking at the wrong woman."
He was referring to an incident that happened in Hofuf in 1978.

The Hofuf Incident:

Hofuf is an ancient town located between Dhahran and
Riyadh. The town is a large oasis that has been a center of desert
trade since trade began. The potters who live in caves nearby are
said to have been there for over five thousand years (their
ancestors, anyway). The town is a collage of many ages. The
caves predate the pyramids. The Turkish fort in the center of
town is over 400 years old. There are artesian wells that are said
to have flowed even before men made homes in the caves. To
my Western eyes, the town appeared in every way to be exactly
the kind of place you might read about in *1001 Arabian Nights.*

In the summer of 1978, three Filipino men, who were pipe
fitters at ARAMCO in Dhahran, went to Hofuf to spend a quiet
Thursday wandering through the old suik. (The Saudi workweek
is Saturday through Wednesday.) While walking through the
narrow dirt streets, they passed by a house with an open window.
From the window, a female voice spoke to them in English.
From what I heard secondhand, the woman talked to them for a
few minutes and then invited them in to get a drink of water.
Unknown to both the woman and the three men, a Mutawwi'un
was watching. When the men came out of the house, they were
immediately arrested by several Mutawwi'un and taken to the
local jail. The woman was also arrested. After many hours of
interrogation, the woman and all three Filipinos supposedly
confessed to adultery. The following day, immediately after
Mosque, The woman was buried up to her waist in the sand and
stoned. The three men where taken to the center of town where
their heads were lopped off with a sword.

In Saudi Arabia, Islam is the state religion and the Holy
Quoran provides the written law. These Holy Scriptures are
considered to be the absolute word of God. Quoranic law is
known as Shareea. About 90-some-years after the death of The
Prophet Mohammed, his followers wrote down his teachings.

The compilations of these writings are the Holy Quoran. Since these writings are still in their original language and were written relatively soon after the prophet's death, it is believed that his words have not been altered. In view of how modern-day keepers of the flock administer the law, though, I think the message the prophet Mohammed delivered has been paraphrased a bit to fit the ambitions and imaginings of some of those who now call themselves holy men.

The Mutawwi'un mean well when they influence the King to make a decree stating that newspapers, which by law must have quotations from the Holy Quoran, cannot be thrown away or burned. Their intent is pure when they outlaw all other religions. Who can blame them for jailing anyone who conducts a non-Muslim service? Is it so unreasonable that anyone talking to Saudi citizens about any other religion must be stoned, whipped or deported? Is it not in the name of modesty that they force all women beyond the age of puberty to cover their entire bodies with a shapeless black abaaya? Surely everyone knows why boys and girls must be kept apart and sent to separate schools. When the citizens of Saudi Arabia are not able to think and act correctly, who but the Mutawwi'un are there to provide guidance? Weekly executions and dismemberments go a long way toward inspiring correct thinking.

I can accept that the Quoran may be God's will as spoken through The Prophet. I can certainly see God's love in Muslims like Abdul Wahed. I can even go along with praying five times a day—that's actually a good thing. The only difficulty I have with Islam is how it's enforced. I have trouble believing that God wants an army of terminators keeping his children in line.

"Pray!—or I'll be back."

Killer Camels From Kuwait

Water Melon Stands in Katif

Old Turkish Fort Near Al Hofuf

BEST FRIENDS

Steve was a ruddy-faced guy with a full black beard, curly black hair and a perpetual mischievous grin. He wore sandals and jeans to work no matter what the occasion. He listened to and told stories with equal enthusiasm. He found humor in everything and used it to pull smiles from the depressed.

When we met, I did most of the talking. I was suffering from jet lag and new-world euphoria, so he just listened and grinned. After rambling for fifteen minutes, I mentioned that I was headed to the personnel office for processing. Steve offered a ride.

I was amazed at how familiar he was with the personnel office. He knew where to go, whom to see, what forms to fill out, and the right answers to key questions. After maneuvering through the personnel office, Steve took me to the ID-card office. The line appeared to be several hours long.

"Follow me," Steve said, "I know the guy that's in charge."

We went through a side door in plain sight of the line. Once inside, Steve walked over and had a private conversation with the man taking the pictures. The photographer motioned for me to come over. He showed me where to stand, changed the background to a different color, and took my picture. Ten minutes later, I had my new laminated ID card.

I moved into my new office the following day. Steve came by and took me to lunch. After lunch, we toured company facilities. I asked how he knew his way around the company so well. "Oh, I've lived here awhile," he said, "and I just know a lot of people."

The next day, I had lunch with some other guys from the office. We were each issued a blank receipt card as we entered the dining hall. Everyone showed their ID's and received cards with a thick black strip down the middle. I received a card with no stripe. One of my new friends said, "Hey, how do you rate?"

At the cash register, I discovered that the guys with one stripe had to pay a fifteen-Riyal surcharge (about $5.00). I paid no surcharge. One of my new friends explained how only ARAMCO employees pay no surcharge. He explained how ARAMCO society is based on a caste system. At the top are the ARAMCO executives. They live in castle-like homes, have servants, get special privileges and make an obscene amount of money. Then there are the regular ARAMCO employees. They live in nice homes, get special privileges and make good salaries. Below them are the contractors. Contractors live in facilities provided by their company. Probably because they get a lot of the real work done, they are almost equal to the Aramcons. At the bottom of the barrel are the servorgs (an acronym for service organization personnel).

Servorgs live in ARAMCO housing or ARAMCO-contracted off-site housing. They use ARAMCO vehicles and may use some ARAMCO facilities, albeit with a surcharge. They often make more money than Aramcons. They are usually on short-term contracts and are not part of the ARAMCO community. Perhaps, because of the salary differential and the short-term contracts, most servorgs are considered to be carpetbaggers. Everyone at our table was a servorg (enunciated with disdain by Aramcons).

I thought the man distributing cards just made a mistake and gave me an Aramcon receipt. When it happened again at breakfast the next day, I suspected it had to do with my ID card. I asked a fellow servorg to show me his ID card. His had a different background color. Somehow, I had been issued an Aramcon ID card. It gave me access to the ARAMCO library, shop facilities, movie theater, bowling alley, swimming pool and several other facilities. My servorg buddies could use only the library and the dining hall.

I thanked Steve for his help with the ID card and asked how he did it. He said, "You just have to know the right people." He then grinned and added, "I knew we would be working together and thought it best if we each had the same privileges."

A month went by, and Steve and I became close friends. We worked on the same projects, went to parties, went sightseeing in restricted areas and just enjoyed each other's company. He spoke lovingly of his family and of growing up in the Middle East. I spoke of my family and of growing up in the Midwest. We were each blessed with good parents and each had a mischievous childhood. About six weeks after arriving in Dhahran, I read an ARAMCO magazine and saw a picture of ARAMCO's Chairman. His last name was the same as Steve's. Could they be related? When I saw Steve, I asked him.

"Oh yah, that's my dad," he said rather casually.

"What?" I said. "You mean your dad is the top executive of the world's biggest oil company and you never mentioned it?"

"You never asked," he said with one of those half-smiles.

Steve knew we would not have become real friends if I had known of his father. He wanted me to know who he really was. He wanted friendship without expectations. There were many who were friends with the son of the chairman—not friends with Steve. His other friends, who only knew the son of the chairman, were selling themselves short.

Once I knew who his father was, he started introducing me to his other friends. Socializing in the right circles improved my lifestyle. Besides being invited to better parties, I was also asked to housesit from time to time. Steve's friends, who were mostly management-class Aramcons, went on vacation for six-week periods. It was not uncommon to housesit a 5,000-square-foot house. Sometimes the people left their servants to do the housework. The only thing I had to do was feed the cat.

Our social calendar was full, but neither Steve nor I enjoyed partying. What we really had in common was a love for adventure. We each had an insatiable passion for exploring archeological and geological sites. Steve knew where all the really cool places were.

We drove to a rather ordinary stretch of desert one weekend. The site was about 500 yards from the Arabian Gulf. Steve got out two shovels and two buckets. He handed me one of each and started digging.

"What are we digging for?" I asked.

"You'll know when we find one," he replied.

Within an hour, we each had a bucket full of crystalline sand formations that Steve called "Sand Roses." The incredibly beautiful formations looked like a sculpted stone rose. Most were dark gray and had the texture of smooth sandstone. A few were tan. They were formed about two to three feet below the surface where seawater cycled through the sand as tides rose and fell. Steve claimed it had something to do with electrolysis. He explained the formation process, but I don't remember it.

One weekend, we drove a company truck to several old Turkish forts. Some of the forts were over 400 years old. Many of them only needed men and guns to be very defendable. The walls were about 16-feet thick at the base, tapering to about 4-feet thick at the top. The corner towers were around 35-feet tall with the connecting walls being about 20-feet tall. There were elevated walkways behind each wall with gun ports every 5 or 6 feet. It reminded me of the forts in the old westerns. The difference being that the Turkish forts were made of adobe. They used palm logs, palm fronds and palm staves for the roofing and upper flooring. It was amazing how well preserved most sites were. The National Guard was still using one larger fort in Hofuf.

One day, Steve asked, "Would you like to see a lost pyramid as old as the pyramids in Egypt?"

That weekend, we took a four-wheel-drive truck off-road to a remote area. Right in the middle of nowhere was a small sandstone pyramid structure that looked more like the pyramids in Mexico than the pyramids in Egypt. It was buried in the sand except for the top 15 feet. Two cover stones had been removed to expose a passageway that ran completely through and out the other side. In the middle, there were side chambers with tombs. The graves had been robbed long before we arrived. We found ten desecrated chambers. The only objects left inside were empty Sohat® water bottles and empty Pepsi® cans.

The most amazing thing was the limestone blockwork laid without mortar. The blocks fit so tightly together that my business card would not fit between any two. According to Steve, ARAMCO-sponsored archeologists dated the site at around 3,000 BC. The structure was covered by sand until an ARAMCO survey crew found it. Steve did not know who built it or what happened to its contents.

A few months later, we went back for a better look. More of the structure had been exposed, but we couldn't get to it. A very tall, very secure, barb-wire-topped cyclone fence had been erected around it. There was a large sign in English and Arabic bolted to the gate. It read, "Property of the Ministry of Saudi Arabian Antiquities." It didn't say what they would do to trespassers, but considering local traditions, we decided to keep our bolt cutters in the toolbox.

One of the cool places Steve liked to frequent was the Al Hasa Oasis at Hofuf. Getting there was half the fun. Driving from Dhahran toward Riyadh, the road passes through some of the most bizarre rock formations. The hills look very much like the sandstone hills in Southern Utah except these have more wear. There are wind-worn columns and rock walls with holes worn through. It would be a great movie set for an alien world. We made several trips there to hike around, over, under and through an ever-changing sandstone and limestone maze.

One weekend, we made it past the rock formations and actually arrived at the Al Hasa Oasis. We were driving down a road lined with huge rock monuments. We turned a corner and saw nothing but palm trees all the way to the horizon. Steve said there were over 25,000 acres of irrigated trees. A little farther down the road, we stopped at an ancient well that supplied water to the trees.

I have seen a lot of wells but never one like this. It was an artesian flow from a 100-foot-diameter hole that ancient craftsmen had cut through solid limestone. From the surface to as far down as one could see, the well was lined with precision-cut stone very much like the stone at the tomb. The water was warm and clear. Water flowed from the well directly into a 50-foot-wide irrigation cannel. The well had a flow of at least 500-million gallons per day. It was virtually a river coming right out of the ground. No one knew how old it was or who constructed it.

The Al Hasa Oasis is what life was about in Saudi Arabia before oil. Most Westerners think of Saudi Arabia as the land of Arabs, camels and sand. The truth is, neither the Arabs nor the camels like the sand all that much. They each prefer to live in the shade with plentiful food and water. No one actually lives in the desert. They just pass through it on their way from one green place to another green place. The Al Hasa Oasis is one very green place.

Another false image in the West is the icon of an oasis as a small watering hole with a few palm trees around it. The Al Hasa Oasis is more like a vast tropical jungle. It is a world of date palms, banana palms, green parrots, monkeys, wild cats, foxes, and a few poisonous vipers.

Around another bend, just on the edge of the Oasis, is a large hill riddled with caves. There is a small community of potters living in the lower caves. Archeologists believe the potters have lived there for over 5,000 years. It would be interesting to know their true lineage. A Saudi from Damam told me the Hofuf potters were once Jews. They don't look like other Saudis, so who knows?

Their cave homes were closed off in front with whatever materials were handy. Some used wood, some used stone, and some used palm fronds over a palm-stave framework. Their shops are in front of their caves. Split palm-logs support a flat palm-thatched roof. Their potting wheels and clay are kept under the shade structure. Their pots and bowls are stored and displayed in front of their shops. They live an ancient lifestyle that has changed little in 5,000 years.

After haggling over a few bowls, we drove into the village of Hofuf. It is a trading village built outside of a garrison-size Turkish fort. All the buildings are adobe and Split-palm-log construction. All the streets are narrow, dirt, and rarely run straight for more than a hundred feet. The village is one big suik with shops in front of every home. Meat, fruits, and vegetables are all displayed outdoors under palm-frond shade structures. Large goatskin water bags are hung in the shade. The moisture evaporating through the skins keeps the water cool. They work better than the plastic water coolers used by Westerners.

At 10 AM the streets are crowded. The ratio of donkey carts to Toyota pickups is about one to two. The ratio of goats to Westerners is about one to one. The din of deals being made, horns honking and goats bleating is broken only by the blare of prayer call—but the goats keep bleating.

I bought one of those curved Arab daggers. I found out later it was made in India specifically for gullible tourists. Steve bought a small bag of dates. We passed by the meat market and wondered if the flies on the hanging meat were laying eggs. The smell of a nearby rotting dead donkey further dissuaded us from buying the meat. We left when a large government tank truck came down the street spraying everything and everyone with a cloud of DDT. It was a Rudyard Kipling kind of days.

A month later, we returned for a different kind of adventure. Steve knew of a large cave that was said to rival Carlsbad Caverns. We found it without much effort. There were quite a few people going into and coming out of the cave. The entrance was about twenty-feet wide and about sixty-feet high. There was Arabic graffiti everywhere. We were disappointed because of the crowd, but since we had food, water and two flashlights each, we decided to go in.

The cave had been formed by water but was now dry. Most of the stalactites and stalagmites had been removed. The floor of the cave was relatively flat for the first two hundred yards. People were not venturing farther because the cave became dark and narrow. Up to that point, the cave fairly reeked of urine and fecal matter. You really had to watch your step. We decided to go deeper. From that point on, walking was more difficult, but the bad odor was gone. We had to climb up in some areas and down in others. Some passageways opened into large rooms with flat floors. Other passageways either dead-ended or tapered down so small that we couldn't pass. Whenever we came to a room with more than one exit, we took the one that looked most promising. To get from one medium-size room to a more spectacular big room, we had to crawl on our sides for about 50 feet through a narrow vertical slit. We stopped to rest and eat lunch in the big room. We had been crawling, crouching and squirming for over four hours.

Since we were just sitting there, we decided to shut our lights off to save the batteries. We figured our eyes would adjust to the darkness. They didn't. We turned one light back on.

We sat eating our sandwiches. We began contemplating what we had done, where we were, and where we might go next. Up to that point, we had been driven completely by euphoria. Now, common sense was kicking in. It occurred to us that we had not told a sole of our plans. We had traveled at least a mile underground. We had not marked our turns at the multiple-choice junctions. The flashlights we were using were getting dim. A speedy retreat seemed logical.

We started back with a sense of foreboding. The fifty-foot slit seemed twice as long and half as wide. Halfway through the slit, Steve's first flashlight failed. When he lit his second light, my light appeared so dim that I lit my second light, too. We were exhausted and moving slower. We had no idea where a wrong passage might lead. Then I had to go and verbalize a thought.

"Uh, what happens if we have an earthquake?"

"Just keep crawling," Steve said reassuringly. He then started crawling much faster. It was extremely difficult to move quickly through a vertical slit the same width as my own body. As we neared the medium-sized room, it felt as if the slit were constricting. The air seemed thinner, and I began hyperventilating. We stopped at the medium-sized room so that I could catch my breath. We were thousands of feet below the surface and were unsure of the way out.

"Let's think about something else," Steve suggested. He then began talking about the girl he had been in love with since his early teens. His talking helped me get control, but that sense of foreboding wouldn't go away. For the next four hours, Steve talked about his one true love and I talked about my wife. We made all the right turns and emerged with a good fifteen-minutes of flashlight left. Piece of cake.

After that experience, we were best friends. We shared stories about our lives that neither of us would want published. Mostly, though, Steve talked about that girl. I told him that he was obsessed. He told me I would understand if I met her. A month later I had my chance.

I met Steve at a small party. There was a good-looking girl with Steve, but she didn't seem interested in him. In fact, it was not apparent that she even liked him. Later, I told Steve he was headed for a heartbreak with such an out-of-balance relationship. It made him angry. Truth does that. A week later, I left Dhahran for a temporary assignment in the States.

I tried to contact Steve a few times but never made voice contact. I received a few letters and sent a few, but neither of us stood still long enough to meet anywhere. The last I heard was that he was getting married to that girl and that they might live in Dhahran. I would have sent a wedding gift, but I wasn't sure where to send it.

When I returned to Saudi Arabia, I was living on the other side of the country in Yanbu. It was nearly five years before I returned to Dhahran. I went to my old office and found one friend still working there. I asked him where Steve was hanging out. His smile faded.

"Nobody told you?"

"Nobody told me what?" I replied with apprehension.

"Jeezzz, I'm sorry," he said, "Steve is dead."

The words crashed into my head like the bullet that had ended my friend's life. The details and the imagined motives only made it worse. I wrestled with the thought that if I had been there for him I could have helped fight the darkness. After all, that's what friends do, right?

Everyone meets death sooner or later. It gets our relatives. It gets our friends. It gets us. Faith stops the fear, but it doesn't stop the grief. I miss my friend. He provided so much light when my life was dark. Somewhere, his light still shines. I will see it again—probably at the end of some tunnel.

Killer Camels From Kuwait

Christopher A. Larsen

The Old Way to Get There

GETTING THERE

There are only three reasons for going to Saudi Arabia: you have orders, you are running away, or you are a Saudi. I had neither orders nor a Saudi passport.

I signed a short-term contract to work at the Arabian American Oil Company (ARAMCO). The only thing I knew was that it paid well and the job was somewhere on the other side of the world. For an ex-Nebraska-farm-boy, it was an odyssey. It was joining the Foreign Legion, but for more money.

For two weeks, I was wined, dined and indoctrinated by those who hired me. They did their best to prepare me. I was their first recruit for Saudi Arabia, so they knew little more than I did about what to expect. They made sure I had a valid passport with the proper visas, had all my shots and had an international driver's license. Beyond that, they were guessing.

I remember being in the Air France Terminal at JFK International Airport waiting for my first flight on a 747 and my first trip across the ocean. I had two suitcases, a wallet full of company credit cards and almost enough cash. As instructed by my boss, I kept my passport and wallet in my front pants pocket.

The 737 to JFK was uncomfortable. The seats were narrow and bunched together. There was no legroom. When the lady in front moved her seat back, my knees were locked into her seat for the next several hours. Knowing no better, I had accepted a middle seat. The men on either side were too wide for their seats. They were bold; I was meek. I sat with my arms scrunched in front of me and my hands clasped between my legs.

The Air France 747 was much better. It was taller and wider inside. Two wide isles broke up the twelve seats in each row. You could stand up at your seat without hitting your head, and you could walk down the isle without being chased back by a serving cart. The seats were wider, too, and they had more legroom. The 737 was an overcrowded bus with seat belts. The

747 was a deluxe theater with reclining seats. Even the stewardesses were more attractive.

I managed to get a window seat. The guy in the middle seat was a businessman from Amsterdam. He told me his life's story and I told him mine. During the several hours we talked, we became such good friends. We exchanged addresses and phone numbers. He invited me to spend time with his family in Holland. I promised I would. Neither of us ever contacted the other again.

New York to Paris took more than twice as long as Omaha to New York. It seemed shorter. I watched a good movie and listened to a little soft music—all facilitated by a cheap, uncomfortable plastic headset. (Plastic tubes that stick in your ears? Who's low-tech idea was that?) In contrast to the headset, the food was excellent—French airline, you know.

The cloudy afternoon quickly faded into a clear night. From six miles up, I could see every ship below. The nearly full moon so brightly lit the sea that you could actually make out shapes on the deck of one large ship. Though the sea looked smooth, I knew from the dispersed reflection of the moon that it was not as smooth as the air at thirty thousand feet. The muted whine of four Rolls Royce jet engines droned me to sleep.

A stewardess asking me to put my seat forward brought me to a conscious state. We landed and deplaned. Trusting those in front, I followed the crowd through baggage and customs. My contact in Paris was waiting with a large sign with my name. I had gone to sleep as a naïve farm boy and awoke as an international traveler—albeit a naïve international traveler.

The two weeks of additional training I received in France went quickly. The company guys in France were even better at wining and dining than their American counterparts. A typical lunch was taken on the grounds of a château (French for castle). We would have wine and appetizers, wine and main courses, wine and a salad, wine and a desert, and then wine, cheese and bread. Lunches always lasted three hours. Dinners were a repeat of lunch except with more main dishes.

Prior to my arrival in France, I didn't drink. Although I don't remember actually being drunk in Paris, I don't remember actually being sober, either. My wine-induced euphoria improved my interactions with the French. Anti-American rudeness was taken as humor. It was a bright spot in my life for which I have a somewhat dim memory.

My hosts in Paris took me out for one last long lunch before dropping me at the airport. Unfortunately, by the time they dropped me at Charles DeGalle International Airport, my plane had departed. By the time I realized my situation, my friends had also departed. To make matters worse, I had lost the name and number for my contact in Saudi Arabia. In panic, I asked the Air France agent to get me on the very next flight to Dhahran. She said it was possible to get me there four hours later than scheduled if I took Air France to Beirut and connected with MEA to Dhahran. I did not know what MEA stood for, and I wasn't sure if Beirut was a country or a city. I assumed it must be somewhere between Paris and Dhahran. I could only hope the man that was supposed to meet me was very patient.

"I'll take it," I said, as if I knew exactly what I was doing.

"Are you sure?" she said.

"Yes, I need to meet someone, and I don't want to keep them waiting," I responded with mock confidence. I assumed her concern was for my schedule or for my not getting enough sleep. I further assumed the pretty French girl was just doing her duty in looking after the comfort of an Air France patron. She assumed that I knew there was a civil war in progress in Beirut but didn't care. I have since decided that the road to hell is paved with false assumptions—not good intentions.

The Air France flight to Beirut was similar to the transatlantic flight except that I was the only American on the plane. As I remember, there were not a lot of Europeans onboard, either. Actually, the plane was almost empty. There was no one near me who looked as if they could speak English (another assumption), so I slept.

As the plane descended toward Beirut, a sliver of a moon cast a dim light onto the surface below. I noticed the sea and guessed correctly that it was the Mediterranean. As we turned to final approach, I could see mountains. Then, I could see buildings at the base of the mountains. As we descended, I noticed that many of the buildings appeared to be somehow damaged. As I looked closer, it appeared they might have been shelled. Then, as we crossed the boundary lights of the runway, I could distinctly see gun emplacements—large sandbag circles with antiaircraft guns hiding inside. My eyes widened.

The plane landed and taxied to a dark corner of the airport. The engines throttled down and we sat. It occurred to me then that it was too dark. Most airports are so well lighted that you can read a book with just the background light. This place was as dark as a country road. None of the other passengers seemed alarmed. Everyone just sat quietly.

Above the sound of the idling jet engines, I heard trucks. Then I heard trucks stop near the plane. A stewardess opened the door near my seat. I watched as someone on the ground pushed an old boarding stairway up to the plane. In a few minutes, we were all standing on the ground near the rear of three small furniture vans—the kind you would rent from U-Haul™. I couldn't be sure in the low light, but the trucks appeared to be unmarked. Besides the three trucks, there were six soldiers with what appeared to be AK-47's with large banana clips.

The men with the guns opened the back of each truck and pulled down the loading ramps. We all boarded in silence. When we were all standing inside, the soldiers closed the back of the trucks. I believe they rode outside on the bumper. It was difficult to see anything once they closed the back door. There were no windows in the truck and only a single 12-volt bulb at the front that provided marginal light. Everyone else seemed undisturbed by what was going on, so I figured I'd just go with the flow. I did wonder, though, where they were taking us.

The trucks drove for fifteen minutes then stopped. I heard some Arabic conversation outside, and then the door opened. There was more light here—and more soldiers. We were all unloaded next to what appeared to be a control tower with a small, well-lighted boarding lounge just below. I also noticed that each soldier carried his gun at the ready with his trigger finger resting inside the trigger guard. It was warm there—but that didn't fully explain the sweat rings under my arms that had now reached my waist.

I followed the rest of the group into the building. Some of the passengers were singled out and taken into another room. I found out later that those passengers were strip-searched. Everything we carried was thoroughly inspected. Even baggage that had been checked through to the final destination was deplaned and searched. After making it through the show-and-tell line, I found myself in the well-lighted departure lounge. The few European-looking passengers that were on the inbound flight were nowhere to be seen. Beirut had been their destination. The remaining passengers were waiting for the MEA flight to Dhahran. I was the only one in the room with non-Arabic clothing. Finding Waldo in that crowd was pretty easy.

I sat there assuming that people that looked and smelled so radically different most certainly could not speak English. I sat there listening to their strange-sounding conversations, not really knowing where I was or even if I was in the right place. Out of desperation, I asked a young Saudi man if we were in the right place to wait for the MEA flight to Dhahran. I expected either a blank look or a "Me no speak English," response. To my pleasant surprise, the young man not only spoke English well, he spoke it with an English accent.

The Saudi was both friendly and helpful. We spoke only briefly before the trucks came to take us back to the dark end of the runway. We talked just long enough for me to be reassured that I was in the right place waiting for the right airplane. I learned that MEA stood for Middle Eastern Airlines and that

English was the de facto commercial language in Saudi Arabia. He also taught me how to say, "Me no speak Arabic," in pigeon Arabic.

The ride to the MEA plane was less intimidating—something about knowing where they're taking you. Standing tightly packed into those close quarters, I realized that my fellow passengers could be divided into two distinct groups—those who did not know what a bath was and those who took baths in perfume. The combined aroma was anything but a neutral scent.

The MEA flight was a 737. There were no assigned seats, but since I was one of the first on the plane, I managed to get a nice isle seat near the rear. Both seats next to me were empty. Just as I was counting my blessings, a late boarder, an old Saudi man with a falcon perched on his leather-clad arm, was escorted back to my row and was seated in the window seat. The stewardess then brought a perch on a stand back and placed it in the seat between the old man and me. The bird was then transferred to the perch. Even though the falcon was shrouded, I sat leaning slightly into the isle.

The plane blasted off at a very steep angle. I hoped the fast climbing rate was necessary to avoid the mountains and not to avoid hostile fire. Since everyone seemed relaxed, I decided it was the mountains. Two minutes after the landing gear left the tarmac, the no-smoking light went out with a loud "ding." Seconds later, everyone except me lit up a cigarette. In less than a minute, the plane was so full of smoke that I could not see all the way to the front. I found myself wishing for some hostile fire—just one or two bullets—just enough to make the pilot turn the no-smoking sign back on.

Once we leveled off, an old man who had been sitting in front of me took his carryon bag into the isle. He squatted down and took out a portable cook stove and one of those odd coffee pots. He was trying to light the burner when a stewardess saw him. After a rather loud exchange, the man reluctantly put his stove away and went back to his seat. As I nodded off, I thought

I heard the distinct "baaahhh" of a goat. Later, as everyone deplaned, I looked for the goat but did not see one.

When we finally landed in Dhahran, at 1 AM, I noticed an Air France 747 near the terminal. There were two other 747's there, also: a British Air and a KLM plane. I decided that the Air France plane was the one that I would have been on. "Not too late," I thought. I was too tired to do the math on how many people those three planes held—and I was too tired to realize that all of them were in front of me. I let everyone else scramble off of the plane ahead of me. "Why rush?" I remember thinking. "I'm here, and my contact will be waiting for me."

Upon deplaning, I realized why everyone else had fought their way to the door. I found myself at the rear of a line that extended for several hundred yards (those parked 747's were only a few of the planes that had landed that night). An hour later, after making it to the front of the health-certificate line, I found myself at the rear of an equally long passport-stamping line. By the time my passport was stamped, it was after 3 AM. The corridor leading away from the passport windows, led into a room about the size of a large gymnasium—the baggage collection area.

Dhahran Airport in 1977 did not have modern turnstile baggage handling equipment. They had an agricultural conveyor belt system that dumped bags from all the planes into one large twenty-foot-high pile. Then, for a price, there were a dozen or so large Pakistani labors standing by to help you sort through the pile for your luggage. Once you found what was left of your luggage, you then lugged it through the longest line of all, the customs line.

By the time I made it to the customs table with my two suitcases and my carryon, I was exhausted and in no mood to be hassled any further. The teen-age Saudi customs agent who went through my bags couldn't find anything to confiscate, but he did hold out his hand as if to receive some compensation for not hassling me. He caught me at a bad moment. In a rather loud, angry voice, I blurted, "You want Money? How much money do you want?" The young man looked sheepishly from side to side; his face reddened and he motioned me on.

I cleared customs at 4:30 AM. I walked up the ramp to the area where everyone holds up signs. There were many signs, but not one for me. To make matters worse, I had arrived during Hajj. I didn't know it then, but sane people do not enter Saudi Arabia during Hajj. During that holy period, Muslims from all over the world make their pilgrimage to Mecca. As I made my way through the airport looking for anyone who might be from ARAMCO, I had to step over or around the sleeping bodies of hundreds of Hajjis who were spending their first night in Dhahran on the marble floor of the airport arrival lounge.

In complete bewilderment, I wondered through the airport looking for anyone who might help me. The architecture, the people, the sounds and smells—everything was foreign. It occurred to me that I was 9,000 miles from home, had no local coinage and no phone number to call even if I could find a phone. I didn't even know whom I was supposed to meet. It also occurred to me that the only thing I had learned to say in the local language was, "Me no speak Arabic." Bewilderment degraded to a sense of doom.

Then, at 5 AM, after wandering all the way to the other end of the airport, I saw a small sign that read, "ARAMCO Office." I felt redeemed. I thought I heard angels singing, but it turned out to be a flock of noisy sparrows flying through the interior of the departure lounge. I walked over to the door. It was locked. But wait, there was a note. The note had my name on it. There was also an ARAMCO phone on the wall that didn't require coins. Maybe that singing wasn't just birds.

The note gave me the number of a Mr. John Kriesmer. Never mind that it was 5 AM, I called him. He sounded tired but told me to wait outside and he'd be right down. At 5:45 AM, on a Thursday morning (the equivalent of our Saturday morning), I met John Kriesmer and his son. I was so grateful to see the guy. John was friendly but a bit distracted. He drove me back to ARAMCO headquarters and got me a room at Steineke Hall (the guest facilities usually reserved for visiting executives).   John told me to sleep in and he would send someone to pick me up around lunch. He looked as if he really wanted to get back to his own bed. I thanked him profusely and said goodnight even though the sun was just rising.

The next day I learned that John was the Director of Community Services and my new boss. I also found out that he had been sick in bed with the flu when I called.   First impressions out of the way, I was off to a good start.   Who would have ever guessed that running away would be so much fun.

Steineke Hall in Dhahran

The Dhahran Kitchen Before The Sewer Pipe Broke

A PLACE TO SLEEP

When I was ten, I wanted to know why we didn't live in a house like the big one on the hill. Mom scolded me and told me to be thankful for the home we had. She sat me down and told me of other little boys who lived in tin shacks, of other little boys who lived in cardboard boxes, and of other little boys who lived in caves dug into cliffs beside a river bank. I loved it when she told me those stories, but I knew she was just kidding. Even after she showed me a picture of a little boy in front of a cave that had been dug into a riverside cliff—a full-color photo from her brother's *National Geographic* magazine—her stories were still just fairy tales.

Twenty years later, I was living in a company-leased flat in Al Khobar, Saudi Arabia. Reality had become what was once a fake photograph in Uncle Bud's magazine. My apartment was not built into the side of a riverbank, but living there often made me think of those dreadful places an ungrateful little boy might end up. Sometimes I felt that off-site housing was punishment for not believing my mother's stories.

Only two groups of people are assigned off-site housing: those with a minor job in a major company, and those with a major job in a minor company. In nine years as an expatriate, I was always in one of those two groups. I started out with a minor job in a major company—the Arabian American Oil Company.

Americans with major jobs at ARAMCO live well. To attract long-term professional people, ARAMCO builds communities that rival the rich neighborhoods on the hills back home. The idea is to make people too comfortable to leave. Those with minor jobs, on the other hand, get comfort-challenged off-site accommodations. The idea is to minimize the expense of temporary help. Those living in ARAMCO communities are sheltered from the real Arab world; those living off-site are immersed into it—baptized by the local culture.

My first flat in Al Khobar had its amenities. It had marble floors, high ceilings, and was only a block from the Arabian Gulf (Persian Gulf on some maps). It was within easy walking distance of the local shops and was within easy earshot of the megawatt speakers mounted high on the minaret of the nearby mosque. I always knew when to pray.

The first thing I noticed upon moving in was a large, half-inch crack that ran from the ceiling down to floor in my bedroom. I could look through the crack and see the building across the alley. I thought the crack was from an earthquake, but my boss told me otherwise.

"There are no earthquakes in this region," he said. "The area is geologically stable." He suggested filling the crack with silicone and forgetting about it.

I filled the crack, but I could not forget it. I had reoccurring nightmares of a minor earth quake and of being crushed by tons of concrete as first one crack developed, then another, then another, until the whole building just shook itself down into a pile of rubble with me somewhere near the bottom.

Shortly after I moved in, the owner of our six-story building decided to build a twin building next door. As they built, I watched. Each evening I monitored the progress of the building that would be identical to the one I lived in. I saw the undersized, rusty, substandard reinforcing bars. I saw the undersized columns. I saw the slipshod workmanship applied to every aspect of construction. I watched as the block layers mixed their mortar on the ground with local sand and dirt. I watched as blocks were laid without a string line and with no concept of square, level or plumb. When the second building was completed, I understood why my wall was cracked. After that, I worried less about earthquakes and more about my window-unit air conditioner vibrating too much.

Besides the oversized air conditioner that entirely filled the only window in my room, there was one lumpy bed, one desk and chair, one reading lamp, one particleboard portable closet, and one oversized ceiling fan. I supplied a cheap stereo, an

Underwood manual typewriter, and a weight-set with a bench. After a month of trying to sleep on the lumpy mattress, I added a foam pad and a sleeping bag that made the floor more comfortable than the bed.

The air conditioner produced a loud humming noise that helped me get to sleep. Besides providing a monotone drone, it blocked background noise from the neighborhood and mitigated the blare of prayer call. In the winter, the air conditioner doubled as a heat pump. In the spring and fall, I ran it on fan. It broke one night, and the sound of car horns, loud TV's, people arguing on the roof next door, two love-sick cats and a guy in the alley trying to harmonize with prayer call made sleep impossible.

The windowless apartment depressed me. Even though there wasn't anything outside except the wall of the building next door, I thought it would be nice to have at least one window. As I became more depressed, I realized that not having a window meant being able to sleep all weekend without interference from sunlight. It was also good to have a dark room when I wanted to look at slides of my wife and kids. In many ways, my apartment was much like that cave my mother had threatened me with, but my cave had no river for fishing.

I turned the ceiling fan on once; it really pushed a lot of air. I was looking for a knob or something to adjust the motor speed when I noticed a slight wobble in the fan. I turned it off and stood on a chair to investigate. The wobble was caused by one of the blades being slightly bent. On closer examination, I noticed that the fan wasn't bolted to the ceiling. When the ceiling was poured, a bent piece of reinforcing bar had been left exposed in the middle of the room. The fan was attached to that bent reinforcing bar with three wraps of bailing wire—rusted bailing wire. I rearranged my room so that only the foot of my bed was under the fan. I then scrounged several pieces of bailing wire from the construction site next door and secured the fan with about thirty or forty wraps. That night, the fan became part of my dreamscape—added to the earthquakes, the vibrating air conditioner and the crumbling walls.

There were two other bedrooms in the apartment. ARAMCO assigned a German man to one and a French man to the other. We shared a kitchen, a bathroom and a living room. The living room had two comfortable couches, a small coffee table, and a black & white TV perched on a rickety metal stand. The stand had a lower shelf with a neat stack of twenty-odd yellowing paperbacks that were added for ballast. Everyone watched TV at night even though the only American programs on were the cartoon show, *Quick-Draw McGraw*, and ten-year-old reruns of *Little House on the Prairie*. Our other choices were either documentaries about ARAMCO or Islamic religious programs. One of the most exciting moments in our shared living room occurred when the single light bulb that hung from the center of the ceiling exploded and showered the three of us with fragments of glass. As we sat there in total darkness, it struck me that this was one of our brighter moments.

Our bathroom was as large as the living room. It, too, had a single incandescent bulb hanging from the middle of the ceiling. After the living-room incident, I always wore my rubber sandals while showering to avoid the inevitable light-bulb shrapnel.

For such a large bathroom, it had a small shower. A three-foot by three-foot area had been partitioned-off in the corner of the room by hanging a vinyl shower curtain above the floor with the standard rusty bailing wire. The wire was suspended from lag screws driven into the ceiling. The piping for the shower was all galvanized and was fastened directly to the marble-surfaced walls with metal plumber's tape and concrete anchor screws. There were two leaky gate valves that controlled hot and cold water. The shower head, which was eight feet above the floor, was not actually a shower head; it was one of those big round things you put on the end of your hose to water your garden.

The wastewater from the shower and from the sink drained across the sloped surface of the floor to the center of the room. The floor had been poured and finished to slope to the center floor-drain. A four-inch-high concrete threshold had been built at the doorway to keep the living room from flooding. The whole system was dreadfully unsanitary but functional. After brushing your teeth, you had to run a lot of water in the sink before moving your feet. If you didn't, you would track toothpaste and saliva onto the living-room carpet.

Hot water for showers and shaving was supplied by a large electric water heater hung near the ceiling in the adjacent corner of the room. Its metal support bracket rusted through while we were living there, and the whole thing slid down about an inch. If not for the connecting water pipes, it surely would have crashed to the floor. The bailing wire the repairman used to fix it held for the rest of the time we were there.

Since the bathroom had no windows or vents, it became quite foggy when anyone used it. The dark, damp, semi-anaerobic environment was ideal for mold and fungi. We took turns scrubbing the black slime from the shower wall and floor. We had a mutual understanding, though, that cleaning the vinyl shower curtain was beyond our scope of work. We replaced it once, but the new one slimed over within a few weeks.

The water for the apartment was not supplied by pressurized water lines as is common in Europe and in the States. Water from undersized municipal distribution lines dribbled into a cistern in the basement of our building. From there, it was pumped to the roof via six independent centrifugal pumps. On the roof, there were six plastic storage tanks—one for each floor. Each tank had a float valve that kept it from overfilling (most of the time). For everyone on the lower floors, gravity provided them with plenty of pressure. For everyone on the upper floors, there was almost no pressure. Fortunately, our apartment was on a lower floor. In the summer, the City water supply sometimes could not keep up with demand and our water tank ran dry, but only when you were in the shower.

During the summer, we shut off the hot water heater. The water in our tank on the roof solar-heated and became hotter than the water in our water heater. We used the unheated water in the water heater for cold water. We had to remember that the cold valve was now the hot valve and the hot valve was now the cold valve. It was only a problem if you wanted to take a long shower. Once the cool water from the hot water heater was exhausted, both valves then supplied hot water. Instead of the water becoming cooler as you showered, it became warmer.

The kitchen, like the bathroom, had a floor drain in the center of the room. It had the standard single bulb hanging from the ceiling and had all external piping metal-taped to the walls. In addition to the standard galvanized hot and cold water pipes, and located just behind the stove, there was a rusted four-inch sewer pipe that ran from ceiling to floor. A smaller electric hot water heater was hung near the ceiling in the corner above the sink. The kitchen had a tiny frost-producing refrigerator, a minimal stove and oven, a three-shelf cupboard, and a table with two chairs. The two chairs worked out well because our French roommate refused to eat in our kitchen.

One evening, while watching TV, we heard the sound of gushing water coming from the hallway. At first we thought it was the hot water heater in the bathroom. Then we realized the noise was coming from the kitchen. Rudy, my German roommate, ran and switched on the kitchen light and began cussing in German. I was halfway down the hallway when my breathing was involuntarily cut short. The four-inch sewer pipe had burst and all the sewage from the three floors above was flowing onto our kitchen floor. Because the kitchen also had the center floor drain and the raised threshold, the mess was confined to the kitchen. Raw sewage was running across our kitchen floor, down the drain, and back into the unbroken pipe on the floor below. We sealed the kitchen door and then retired for the evening.

The next day, the building owner had the pipe repaired and the kitchen cleaned. The Indian fellows that cleaned up did a marvelous job. I was quite surprised to find that the marble on the kitchen floor was actually white. I had always known it to be a dark brownish-gray. Even though the kitchen smelled better and looked better after the cleanup, we avoided that room for several weeks.

Many of my consultant friends with off-site housing had much nicer apartments. My ARAMCO friends lived in better homes than most people had back home. Whenever self-pity set in, I dispelled it by thinking of the housing provided to the labor-class employees. By contrast, our flat was the big house on the hill.

Contract laborers were hired to replace the now-illegal slave laborers. Of course, the only real difference between a slave laborer and a contract laborer is that slaves don't get to go home after two years. To the average Saudi contractor, laborers are a resource and an expense—nothing more. Making profit means extracting as much work as possible from each man at the least expense. Minimal housing means minimal expense.

The average laborer lives in an apartment similar to the one I lived in. To cut expenses, contractors put more than one person in a room. Twelve to fifteen laborers are crammed into a twelve-foot by twelve-foot room. Four or five three-level bunk beds are jammed into one room with little space to move between them. A wardrobe locker is provided for every three or four laborers. One four-bedroom apartment I visited had fifty-five Shri Lankan laborers in residence. Some contractors provide an air conditioner for each room; some spare the expense.

With over fifty men living in one apartment, tempers are a problem. When everyone in the apartment is from the same country, perhaps the same village, things are manageable. When roommates are from different countries and different cultures, things are explosive.

One contractor had a mixed labor force of Egyptian Muslims and Filipino Christians. He put them all into one eight-bedroom villa. The Filipinos were given the bottom four bedrooms and the Egyptians were given the four upstairs bedrooms. The two groups shared the bathroom, the kitchen and the dining area. They also shared a large marble courtyard that had been built between the buildings. A fifteen-foot-high block perimeter wall surrounded the courtyard.

Within a week of moving in, five of the new residents required emergency medical care. By the end of the month, a sixth man had died. I was told the deceased had died of bad dreams. I always suspected "bad dreams" meant a pillow over the face with a little weight applied.

Since I was sympathetic to their plight and had some influence on their employer, some of the men from each group met with me after work one day. Each was highly put out by the offensive lifestyle of the other group. Each group found the other group's cooking offensive. Each group found the other group's bathroom habits offensive. And each group was absolutely convinced that their group was the injured party. I was not able to do anything for them, but the Saudi living next door to the villa, after growing weary of the noisy conflict, pressured the contractor into renting another villa and splitting the two groups. The worst living conditions I observed, however, were in an undeveloped area near Macaroon Street in Jeddah. A large community of squatters had built a cardboard village made of discarded shipping pallets, cardboard boxes and Styrofoam packing material. There were goats and chickens everywhere. People cooked on the ground with open fires or on cheap propane cooking plates.

The people living in Macarooni Town were made up of Saudi ex-slaves, marginally employed third-world foreigners, and unemployed illegal aliens. Some entered the country on a Hajj visa and stayed on illegally hoping to find work. Some had worked for a large contractor who had fled the country leaving his workers without exit visas and with no way to leave Saudi Arabia. Some were mentally ill. Some were refugees from a war in Ethiopia. Their common bond of poverty held the community together.

Occasionally there would be articles about their plight in the local English-language newspaper.

The government built high-rise housing to mitigate the embarrassing problem. The project ran aground, though, when the government invited local religious leaders to bless the new buildings. After touring the new buildings, the local religious leaders placed a ban on occupancy because the new buildings had only one elevator per building. Their view was that it would not be proper for unmarried men and unmarried women to ride on the same elevator. When I left the country in 1985, the new buildings had been sitting empty for over one year. The poor were still living in cardboard boxes.

I believe there must be at least one Macarooni mother who tells her little boy of a large stone house on a hill. She tells him that if he is ever fortunate enough to go to school, he may live in such a place one day. But that child—he knows better—those are just fairy tales.

A Crystalline Formation Known as A Sand Rose

ABSTINENCE

The odds of finding a girlfriend in Saudi Arabia are about the same as winning the Power Ball. The odds of being able to talk about it are even worse. The native population has completely different mores and values than the West. Looking at local women can get a man jailed and whipped. Touching one may cost him his life. Even a foreign woman risks jail and worse if caught in public or in a car with a man who is not her husband. Being stoned has quite a different meaning in Saudi Arabia than it does in California.

A small number of men are able to bring their wives, but most cannot. For most single-status males, life goes on with a jar of petroleum jelly. For others, though, raw drive pushes them over the edge. Some heterosexual men resort to homosexual acts. Some take up with animals. Some sink into a state of depression that suppresses their normal drive. A few commit suicide. A few rape. Everyone feels the stress, and everyone has a story.

Rudy, my roommate, was working on a project in a remote area near Al Hasa. He heard some laughter on the other side of a thick cluster of palms. He walked over to investigate. While hiding behind the trees, he saw six Yemenis abusing a wild donkey. They had buried the donkey's legs in the sand. Rudy speculated the legs where hobbled first. One man was playing like a stud donkey while the other five where laughing at him. When one man was done, another took his place. Rudy was quite disgusted with the whole incident. He didn't notice if it was a Jack or a Jenny.

Three Filipino plumbers that worked for ARAMCO showed up at the clinic needing medical attention. They all had Gonorrhea. Since none of them had been on vacation recently, the local police were quite interested in where they had contracted the disease. One of the men confessed that he had caught the disease from a blowup rubber doll. One of his friends had brought the sex toy back from the Philippines. He and his friends were sharing. The doll was confiscated. The men were whipped and deported. I never heard what happened to the doll.

Fred, another friend, had a contract similar to mine. Every four months, Fred and I were given two-weeks paid vacation to anywhere in the world we wanted to go. Fred told his wife his vacation was two weeks per year. Once a year, he went home to visit his wife. Twice a year, he went to Bangkok, Thailand. He had a regular girl there. He told me that he sent her money every month. He showed me photos of her that were inappropriate for the family album.

Fred's story is not unique. Perhaps a third of the Western work force and a large number of Saudis make regular trips to Bangkok. The women are beautiful, friendly and affordable. Everyone tells me that the licensed professionals are clean and the only real risk is with the unlicensed streetwalkers. How the professionals manage to stay clean while the streetwalkers become unclean is beyond my comprehension.

The one time I passed through Thailand, I had a four-hour layover in Bangkok. Fortunately, I had taken a *Time* magazine along to read on the plane. The cover story was on AIDS. Any temptation to find out for myself about Bangkok was extinguished by the article. The article told of a medical research team that had recently done a random check of a large number of streetwalkers in Bangkok. Their survey found a 40% HIV infection rate (and that was in the '80's). It concerns me that most of the expatriates who enjoy the pleasures of Bangkok will one day return home bearing gifts.

Over the years, I heard several stories about a secret whorehouse in Dhamam, Saudi Arabia. The idea of such a place existing in a society that executes prostitutes fascinated me. A friend and I became so intrigued by the concept that we decided to track it down (for curiosity purposes only). We clearly understood that using such a facility carried the threat of beheading. We figured we could drive by and see what the place looked like. We decided that if we actually found it, and there was anything or anyone visible from the street, we could risk a spy photo with a right-angle lens. We discretely asked around. Even those that originally told us about it gave us such vague directions that we suspected we were on a Snipe hunt. After a week of spy work, the adventure ended with our conclusion that it was a mythical whorehouse—something on the order of Shang Ri La. Perhaps it is really there, hidden in plain sight. Perhaps, it was our own disbelief that prevented us from seeing it—or maybe it was our guardian angels.

Donald, a consultant to ARAMCO, lived on the third floor of a local Al Khobar apartment building. His balcony overlooked the backyard of a Saudi Family. One day Don caught a glimpse of a Saudi woman in the back yard. She did not have her habia on and looked up. Don caught her glance and gave a quick wave of acknowledgment. She immediately went inside and her husband came out. When Don saw the man, he went back into his own apartment. A few minutes later, the man and two local policemen were at Don's door. Fortunately, Don had the presence of mind to explain to the one police officer who spoke English that he had only accidentally glanced down at the woman and had meant no disrespect. Don apologized profusely to the husband who decided he would accept the apology if Don promised to not look into his yard again. Who knows how long Don would have sat in jail if the man had not accepted the apology. The next week, the man had an angled shade-cloth structure erected that completely blocked his back yard from Don's view.

James, an ARAMCO employee, lived in Al Khobar next to a villa occupied by a large Saudi family. It was a typical four-apartment villa with each apartment occupied by one of the wives and her children. Each apartment was identical except for orientation. I suspect that each had similar if not identical furniture. By law, a man can have four wives, but he must provide equally for each. This particular family had a combined sibling population of at least ten girls and five or six boys. When they all came outside, Jim would say hello to the man and more or less ignore the wives and children.

After Jim had lived there awhile, he noticed one particular Saudi girl, about fifteen or sixteen years old, who would hang around near his truck in the evenings. Shyly, she would wave to him, and nervously, he would wave back. Once, when he was getting into his truck to go to the store, she came up to him and said in clear English, "Hello, how are you?" Not wanting to offend her, he smiled and said, "Hello." To Jim's relief, she giggled and retreated back to the doorway of her villa.

After that, the girl began waiting for him in the morning. She would wave to him and try out a phrase or two as he drove off to work. He confided in a friend who had lived in Arabia for many years. His friend cautioned him to take great care to avoid any further contact with the girl. The long-time resident warned him that it would only take one crazed Mutawwi'un (religious police) to trump up rape or adultery charges against him and he would end up in chop-chop square.

The very next day, he found a note on his windshield. The girl wrote telling him she loved him and wanted to meet him privately. He took the note directly to his boss. That afternoon, several of his company's laborers were sent home with him to help him move to an apartment in another part of the city.

I have heard other such stories where the man was not so wise. When another family member or a Mutawwi'un discovers such activities, the consequences are usually beheading for the man and stoning for the woman. In some cases, one or both parties are shot. In other cases, a brother or father executes the girl. When a family member does the execution, it is done to protect the family name. These legal murders are often done by strangulation or drowning.

Samir, a Lebanese friend, told me you can never win when a Saudi girl decides she wants you. If you do it, you lose your head. If you don't do it, she says you did, and you still lose your head. His advise: "If you find yourself in such a situation, leave the country as quickly as possible."

At ARAMCO facilities there are single British secretaries and single American nurses. That may be the real reason that access to ARAMCO facilities is highly restricted. Of course, single men who do have access to ARAMCO find the competition stiff. There are at least thirty single men to every single female at the average ARAMCO facilities. Many of these women are there for the high pay. Many others are looking for, and find, wealthy husbands. An adventurous few find the evening pay to be better than the day pay. A friend, who occasionally contributed to one woman's after-hours trust fund, told me the going rate was $300 per night for him and $1,000 per night for anyone else (he ended up marrying her). He told me of another woman he knew who only did private parties for select wealthy locals. Her compensation was often over $10,000 per party. Although I never heard of any Western women being executed for prostitution, I believe the risk factor strongly influenced their fees.

Twice, gay Arab men interested in a sexual encounter approached me. Although I have no malice toward homosexuals, I found each incident upsetting. Both times I went home and looked in the mirror to see what it might have been that invited the advance. The most upsetting incident for me, though, was when one of my friends, whom I still believe to be heterosexual, made an advance toward me. It was done in a joking way, but it was clear that he was serious. I made light of the advance and it never happened again. I reminded myself that we were all sexually frustrated. I figured his Vaseline jar was probably empty and let it pass.

Of all the sexually frustrating moments I experienced in the Middle East, the worst was a situation that developed at my apartment in Al Khobar. I shared the apartment with a German and a Frenchman. At first, we all got along—sort of. The German had a great sense of humor, and we became good friends. The Frenchman kept to himself, was somewhat arrogant, and was not interested in our friendship. The German and I tolerated the Frenchman because we didn't have a choice on roommates. However, there are limits to everything.

One evening, we were all sitting around the living room watching old reruns of *Little House on the Prairie*. Suddenly, with no provocation, the Frenchman started criticizing America and Americans. I ignored him and kept watching TV. Out of the corner of my eye, I noticed the German's face getting red. A large vein became visible in the middle of his forehead. Then, in a sudden leap, the German was on his feet directly in front of the Frenchman's chair. "Look!" he shouted, shoving his finger just an inch in front of the Frenchman's nose. "If it hadn't of been for the Americans, we would have beat you in World War II."

The Frenchman went to his room and we continued watching TV. As we watched TV, the German told me of how he spent the last two years of World War II in a French POW camp.

The Frenchman's room was next to mine. The weekend after the TV incident, the German and I came home late from a joint shopping trip. The Frenchman was in his room with the door closed. We put our groceries away and sat for a little TV before bed. As we sat watching TV, we could hear the Frenchman moaning, groaning and whimpering. The German and I looked at each other with concern. We didn't care for the guy, but we didn't wish him any harm. We talked about it and decided to knock on his door to see if he was OK. I went over to his door and was about to knock when it opened. Out from his room and into the bathroom strode a fantastically beautiful, shapely, naked young woman. My knees became weak and I just stood there for a long time with my mouth open. I turned to the German and his expression was a mirror image of my own. As I stood there, she came back out of the bathroom and sauntered back to the Frenchman's room—a few naked inches in front of me. As she slowly closed the door, she gave me one of those looks and smiled. I went back to the couch, sat down, and watched *Islam Today* on TV. That night I dreamed forbidden dreams and of killing the Frenchman.

The next two weekends, the Frenchman brought the woman back again. He became noisier and she became more brazen. The German and I were climbing the walls. About a week later, I saw the woman at the ARAMCO Dhahran facilities. She was with an older man—an ARAMCO executive—her husband. I told the German about it. When the Frenchman came home from work the next day, we cornered him and told him to leave before the next weekend or risk unthinkable consequences. He left the next day.

In almost any other country, the German and I would have made light of our roommate's activities and lived with our own frustrations. But in Saudi Arabia, the issue was not our own sexual frustration; the issue was genuine fear for our lives. One word from the woman's husband or a Saudi neighbor would have guaranteed each of us a Friday afternoon appearance before a cheering crowd in Chop-chop Square. The very real risk of execution left us no choice but to evict the Frenchman—even though he was open to sharing.

Sexual frustration in Saudi Arabia is not just a problem for expatriates. Sexual frustration is a central part of the Saudi culture. No one there likes the way things are, but no one there dare suggest it be any other way. The rich have four and the poor have none—and that's just the male viewpoint. I can only imagine what life is like for Saudi women.

Christopher A. Larsen

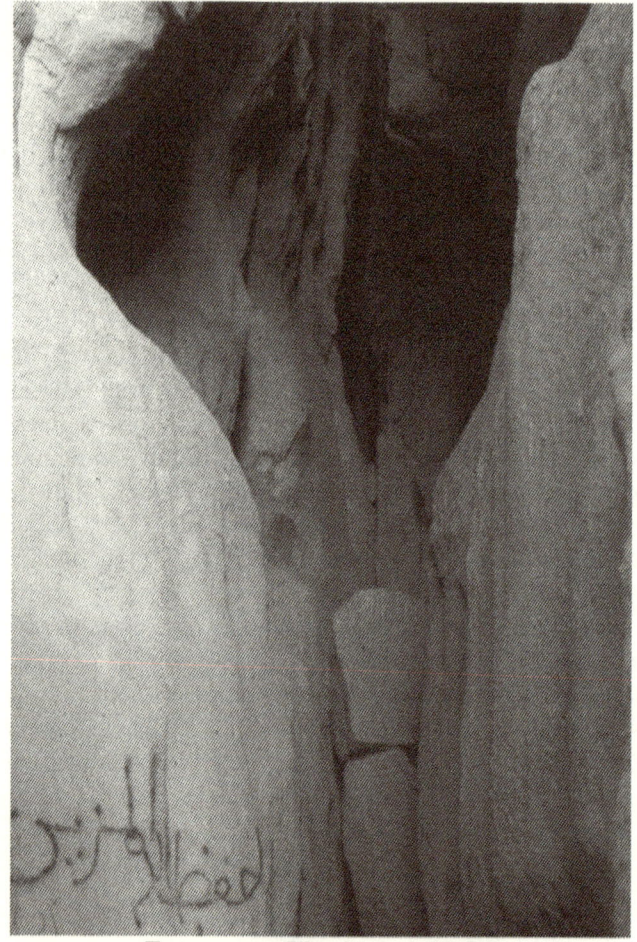

Entrance to The Cave at Hofuf

THE MOTHER OF ALL COCKROACHES

Cockroaches—Yuck!   Scientists will never make me comfortable with the idea of cohabitation. Entomologists say that roaches are not slimy but are actually quite dry to the touch. They would know. Those same scientists say that roaches are more meticulous groomers than a house cat and will actually clean themselves after being touched by a human. I can't dispute their knowledge, but given the choice of which critter will share my bed, I'll take the dirty cat.

Common sense tells us to avoid roaches. They live and breed in sewers. We don't touch things that live and breed in sewers. Truth is, our primal loathing of cockroaches goes way back—way back to before we had sewers. It goes back to when Man lived in caves. It goes back to those dark places in the back of the cave where we only ventured when it was raining too hard to go outside.

It started back in those dark places where our ancestors squatted. I can just see Cain sneaking off to the back of the cave with a hand full of those foot-wide leaves. It's dark. His nose helps him find an area that has not been used recently. He squats and places the leaves next to his left foot. A few minutes later, he grabs the leaves and tries to finish his business. Unknown to Cain, a dozen or so mature roaches have crawled onto the top leaf. Two things happen exactly at that moment: Our primal loathing and disgust for roaches is permanently imprinted into our genetic code, and it becomes taboo in the Middle East to eat with your left hand. Of course, the greatest effect of this event is what happens moments later when Cain explains to Abel just exactly what all the screaming was about.

It is now several thousand years since Cain killed Abel. Man has constructed modern cities all over the Arabian Peninsula—some not far from that original cave. According to local legend, Eve is buried somewhere near Yemen. And buried in the same grave with the mother of all men is the mother of all cockroaches. As with Eve's descendants, many of the mother cockroach's heirs are still living on the Arabian Peninsula.

The average cockroach in Saudi Arabia is about the size of a mouse, only flatter. They are a shiny light-brown color. They have natural body armor that, per gram, is much stronger than steel plate. Anyone weighing less than two hundred pounds cannot crush one with their foot. An insecure stomp just annoys them. Their extremely strong legs are long, angular things with razor-sharp serrated edges. Each leg ends in some kind of Velcro® foot that can firmly grasp any surface—even glass. Their antennae are long, sweeping, tapered wires, constantly in motion. Their eyes and mouthparts are the inspiration for the most dreaded Hollywood monsters. But, the single most evil thing about them is their wings. Under that sleek body armor, they have wings—giant, strong, fully-functional wings.

Over the years, I had many experiences with roaches in the Middle East. Weeding out all the stories of roaches in shoes, underwear, food, etc., two stories are worth telling. The first incident happened the day I moved into a rented villa in Riyadh. The villa had been vacant for several months and everything inside was covered with a thick layer of powder-fine dust. The dust, however, did not explain the putrid stench that overwhelmed me when I first opened the front door. I assumed that the water in the traps for the toilets and sinks had evaporated and allowed methane from the sewer to fill the dwelling. Holding a clean undershirt over my nose and mouth, I ran to the kitchen and turned on the water in the sink. Brown water came out. I ran to the bathroom, turned on the brown water in that sink, turned on the toilet, waited for the reservoir to fill and flushed it. The stench in the bathroom was so bad I almost passed out.

Afraid of losing consciousness, I ran outside and took in large gasps of relatively fresh air. After a few minutes passed, I made a few more short dashes into the building to open windows. A much-needed reprieve came when a Lebanese neighbor came to my front door and made polite conversation for almost an hour. After shaking hands several times with my new neighbor, I reentered the villa. The stench was still present but more tolerable. On closer investigation, I discovered a three-inch-thick layer of dead and decaying roaches covering the entire bottom of my bathtub.

A Filipino friend helped me clean the place. Even after scouring the tub with a whole can of powdered cleanser, and spraying it with at least two cans of disinfectant spray, I still could not bring myself to take a bath in it. A rubber mat purchased at the local suik made showering possible.

A local resident explained the reason for all the dead roaches to me. It has to do with the roach population in the local sewers reaching a critical mass. When this happens, local citizens complain about roaches relocating into kitchens and bedrooms. Local maintenance workers then dump large quantities of DDT into the sewers at strategic locations. The DDT kills millions of roaches. Unfortunately, many of the doomed insects use their fleeting strength to crawl out through any route available. Several thousand of them made it into my bathtub but were not strong enough to crawl out. If my sewer line had been in regular use, only a few of the stronger roaches would have reached my tub. It's a good reason to have someone run water down your sinks and flush your toilets regularly while you are on vacation.

The second encounter occurred several months after moving into a house in Yanbu near the Red Sea. Although the house was clean and certainly not infested, we did find an occasional cockroach. These occasional intruders were always the extra-large mature variety, which we understood to be advance scouts. A can of XXX, outlawed-in-the-States, bug killer prevented them from delivering their reports. We tried to keep the drain entry-points plugged. Sometimes we forgot.

At 5 AM one workday, my alarm ended what was becoming a memorable dream. I yawned, threw my legs over the side of the bed, and forced my semiconscious body to a sitting position. Daily routine led me into the dark bathroom. I automatically positioned myself directly in front of the sink and mirror. Habit then caused my hand to flick-on the light.

There—dead center on the mirror—was a direct descendant of the mother of all cockroaches. With the light now on, we each saw the other at the same moment. Unfortunately for both of us, the roach saw my refection in the mirror and reacted first. It flew away from my reflection. My bare chest blocked its escape. Rapidly beating wings and strong, serrated legs instantly entwined themselves in my chest hair. After an eternal microsecond, I reacted.

My screaming brought my wife into the bathroom. If there had been a 911 number in Yanbu, she would have dialed that first. She feared some horrible monster was attacking me. Most of what actually happened next is blocked from my memory. It's something like being in a car accident and not remembering any of the details. The only eyewitness, however, claims that I was jumping around, flailing at my chest and screaming, "Get it off me! Get it off me!" Eventually, my flailing slew the dreadful beast. I do remember one kicking leg that had to be cut free from my chest hair with a pair of barber shears. I think there was also some greasy yellow stuff smeared across my chest. I took an extra-long shower that morning before going to work.

Entomologists can study them, pet them, play with them and dream about them. It doesn't matter. Nothing they can research, discover or publish will ever convince me that roaches are anything but slimy, dirty sewer demons that belong where their favorite food is plentiful. I'll just keep petting my cat, thank you. My cat knows all about roaches. He eats them.

Killer Camels From Kuwait

Mr. Payne, My Pet Scorpion

Nubian Goats Near Katif (they're everywhere)

PETS

Forget the Society for the Prevention of Cruelty to Animals, forget the Humane Society, and forget the World Wildlife Federation. The exotic animal trade is big in Saudi Arabia. A typical pet store in Jeddah or Riyadh can supply you with any kind of animal. If it's on the endangered species list it's on their call-for-pricing list. The proximity of Africa and India to the Middle East facilitates quick transport from the jungle to the pet store. Some animals arrive legally; some do not. If you can get the money, the pet store can get the animal.

Some wealthy Saudi families have their own private zoos. They typically have several acres of grounds around their villa and a sixteen-foot-high block perimeter wall. In amongst these well-landscaped gardens, non-predatory animals are allowed to roam. Predatory animals are kept in secure cages with barred exercise runs. Those who can afford such zoos can afford a staff to care for them. Although people outside of the Middle East are critical of such private zoos, I personally find them no different than most public zoos in America. A captive animal is a captive animal no matter who may be its keeper.

With so many private zoos and so many privately-owned exotic animals in the Middle East, it is not uncommon for animals to escape. Although not an everyday sight, I have seen an Ostrich trotting down the sidewalk and a Gazelle bounding between cars. The real tragedy, though, happens when middle-class Saudis buy an exotic pet for their kids only to find that they cannot care for it properly. These unfortunate critters are then eaten or abandoned on the street. If they are lucky, they find refuge in a nearby oasis.

Some of the larger oasis areas, such as Al Hasa, Al Karj and Al Hofuf, are populated with exotic animals from both India and Africa. My roommate and I captured a large Green Macaw at Al Karj. Another friend ran into a rather large King Cobra at Al Hofuf. I have seen monkeys, gazelles and many varieties of colorful, noisy birds in these oasis areas. Perhaps these creatures are leftover from when the whole region was a jungle—but that was a very long time ago. More likely, many of these animals were brought into the country as pets.

On one of my little safaris into rural Saudi Arabia, I found a small black kitten. It was an odd-looking little cat. It had extremely large ears and a narrow, elongated head. Its tail and its legs were too long. It was very skinny. But, it purred loudly and was very affectionate, so I took it home to my villa in Riyadh.

The little kitten didn't stay little. The darling thing turned into a much larger cat than I had expected. Not only were its tail and legs too long, its whole body was too long. The adult animal weighed about fifteen pounds. Its short hair and long body, however, made it look thin.

The cat loved me and hated everyone else. When a dog or a stranger startled it, the thing would not hiss as one might expect; the thing would growl. Even though it was my pet, its deep-throated growl always startled me. My neighbor stopped coming over because the cat bit him every time he came through the door.

One day, the cat went outside and didn't come back. I found its collar lying on the welcome mat outside my door. I was never sure if it was my neighbor who killed my cat or if it was the Yemeni exterminators hired by the government.

Yemeni pet mercenaries were hired when the feral cat population became quite large. The local government thought it prudent to exterminate the wild feline. Six months after the Yemeni assassins showed up, you could not find a stray cat anywhere. Six months after the cats disappeared, rats and mice became even more abundant than the cats had been.

Had my cat lived, I would have tried to bring it back to the States. Considering its exotic look and nature, I suspect it would have been difficult getting it through customs. An acquaintance who fancies exotic cats told me it was a Saudi Biting Cat. She claimed such cats came from the natural crossbreeding of domestic Egyptian cats and wild Asian Leopards. I don't know if she knew what she was talking about, but that certainly was a strange cat—and it did bite.

It was a smart cat, though. A few weeks before it was killed, I went to the store to buy the thing some cat food. On the shelf beside the cat food was a box of sardines from Greece. Since the sardines were cheaper than the cat food, I bought the sardines. When I got home, I opened a can, put half the sardines on a plate for the cat and half the sardines on a plate for me. I sat the cat's plate on the floor and placed mine on the table. Being hungry, I ate my sardines rather quickly. Being smart, the cat sniffed his plate, turned around, and went through the same scratching routine that he used in his cat box. I was sick for three days.

Several years later, while living in Yanbu near the Red Sea, I had another experience with a wild Saudi cat. This time, though, it was not pleasant. I had obtained a rather ordinary domestic cat as a pet. One evening, while I was watching my cat play with a cockroach on the marble patio in my back yard, an extremely large, scruffy gray cat jumped from a tree onto my cat's back. It was clear that I would soon lose another cat if I didn't intercede. I grabbed the only thing handy—a long-handled hard-tine garden rake. I brought the rake down on the gray cat's back. He released my cat and backed off a bit. With ears bend back and crouched low, he screamed at me. As I started to raise the rake again, he lunged straight at my face. Reactively, I brought the rake down hard. One of the tines made a hole in the top of the cat's head. Before I could feel guilty about killing a cat, it jumped up and started coming at me again. Then it stopped, turned and jumped up onto and over my six-foot-high block wall.

A few days later, as I was leaving for work, I saw the cat walking on the other side of the street. As soon as it saw me, it turned and ran. I found out later that there were quite a few wild cats in Yanbu. Some of them were just the wild descendants of domestic cats, but others were a local wild cat that some called a Sand Cat. The Sand Cat, from what I am told, is another hybrid between wild and domestic cats. They are quite aggressive and will kill domestic cats and small dogs.

My rather meek domestic cat survived the attack. Unfortunately, she did not survive a jaunt through the nearby Korean construction camp. She went in but did not come back out. I have always wondered if Cat Tempura goes well with Kemchi and rice.

Just before finding my first Saudi cat, I had a pet Black Scorpion. Well, it's probably not fair to call it a pet since I never actually tried petting it. It was, however, quite entertaining. We kept it in a fish aquarium with a well-secured heavy-duty screen cover. We put sand and rocks in the bottom so the critter would feel at home. We fed it cockroaches, flies and any other kind of bug we could catch. Watching it battle a large locust was exciting, but no one would bet on the locust.

One day, I spotted a small, shiny green beetle crossing my floor. I let it crawl up onto a piece of paper and then dropped it into the scorpion's tank. The scorpion scurried over and grabbed the bug with his left pincher. It started moving the beetle toward its mouth but stopped and threw it away. The scorpion repeatedly jammed its left pincher into the sand. It then ran back to the green bug and grabbed it with its right pincher. It threw the bug away again and jammed its right pincher into the sand. Then, it turned over on its back and was still.

We poured water on the scorpion but could not revive it. After two days, it revived itself. We gave the scorpion away, agreed to consciously avoid shiny little green beetles, and decided that a dog might make a more appropriate pet.

There are two species of dogs native to Saudi Arabia. The one kept as a hunting dog is a Saluki. They look like Greyhound to me. The only thing to distinguish a Saluki from a Greyhound is their color. Every Saluki I saw was a light tan color. They seemed to be a mild-mannered dog that did not bark much.

The other native Saudi dog has an Arabic name I cannot pronounce. These ugly dogs look pretty much like a Dingo and are not well liked by the local population. I never saw one of them kept as a pet.   Even though all of them seemed quite friendly (real face lickers), they all lived on the street and ate from the garbage piles that collect behind the back walls of many Saudi homes.

The first time I met one of the semi-wild ugly dogs, I was standing outside of a local grocery store. The dog was prancing around the many shoppers, tail fiercely wagging and tongue slopping from one side of his mouth to the other. He instantly responded to my short whistle. I squatted, and the medium-size dog jumped up on my legs and began licking my face. The locals looked at me with horror and disgust. I thought I had broken some terrible taboo about touching a wild dog—that wasn't it. The people looking on in horror had seen the dog rolling in the rotting remains of a dead donkey just a few minutes earlier. A few seconds later, I figured it out for myself.

Those wild dogs did find favor in the hearts of one group, though. Most of the Asian laborers were more than willing to adopt one or more of those pooches. They would take them to their labor camp, fatten them up, and then serve them at weekend parties. I have been to a few of those parties. Well-spiced dog, washed down with a little aged grape juice is actually quite tasty.

In the '70s, no one seemed to care that large numbers of wild dogs were disappearing. It wasn't until the taste for fresh dog meat led a few enterprising Filipinos to seek out and harvest other breeds—breeds belonging to the American and British employees of ARAMCO. One executive from ARAMCO was quite upset when a Filipino bludgeoned his Labrador right in front of him on the beach at Half-moon Bay. By the time I left the Middle East in the late '80s, it was rare to see a wild dog—and most pet dogs were kept indoors.

Most of the pet dogs owned by American and British people were brought with them from their home country. It was quite easy to bring pets into the county. It was also quite easy to leave with them. However, getting any kind of live animal through US Customs is another matter. Pet lovers who traveled back and forth with their pets told me it all goes smoothly if you have all immunization records, ownership papers and health certificates. Lose a paper; lose a pet.

Besides the real possibility that your pet might be eaten by laborers or confiscated by US Customs, there are other risks to consider when taking a pet to the Middle East. Most of the hotels in the Middle East are not set up to deal with pets. There are no kennels, no pet exercise areas and no pet groomers. The real risk, though, is that your room may not be a safe place to leave your pet.

One family, staying at a major hotel in Riyadh, left their Miniature Poodle in their room when they went down to have breakfast. The hotel was built with a large atrium in the center. All rooms had outside windows and inside windows. The outside windows had a view of the desert. The inside windows had a more desirable view of the well-landscaped atrium. Their room on the tenth-floor had a breathtaking view of the atrium dining room.

As the family was having breakfast in the atrium restaurant, housekeeping was sent to clean their room. When the young Indian man opened the door to their room, the feisty Poodle charged out after him. The surprised Indian man ran. The Poodle tried to turn the corner in hot pursuit. The balcony was paved with shiny, slick marble. There was a wrought Iron railing, but it had a gap of about twelve inches at the base. For an eleven-inch-high Poodle, that was not good news.

The family heard the loud echo of their dog's bark from their table in the atrium. As they looked up, they saw their little pet shoot out from under the rail of their tenth-floor balcony. With mouths wide open, their heads tracked the frantically yipping white ball of fur as it plummeted to its death. The poor little thing splattered right in the center of a table occupied by several Saudi businessmen. After the splat, there was total silence for a few eternal seconds. Then, people were shouting, crying, shrieking and apologizing. My friend Bill, who witnessed this tragedy, did not hang around to see what happened next.

If you find yourself in the Middle East and in need of a pet, adopt a local discard. There are plenty to go around. Love it, care for it, feed it—but don't give it a name. If you give it a name it will be more difficult to give it up when you leave. If your pet has a name, you might take it really personal when you find out that the men in the nearby labor camp have stolen and eaten your beloved Bosco. If you are afraid you might get too attached to a temporary pet, burn your WWF membership card, go to the local pet store and buy an African Lion. You're much less likely to become attached to something that may eat you.

Bedouin's Cargo Truck

Typical Paint Job on A Bedouin's Cargo Truck

IMBIBING

Alcohol is illegal in Saudi Arabia. If caught with alcohol, you go to jail. If you're lucky, after a week or so in jail, you are deported. If you are not lucky, you get forty or more lashes in the public square and then serve a prison sentence of up to five years. An alcohol-related traffic fatality carries the death penalty. In spite of the risk, and probably because of it, most expatriates drink.

There are no bars, nightclubs or liquor stores. Unless you are able to enter Saudi Arabia without passing through customs, there are only three ways to obtain alcohol: Make it yourself, buy it from someone else who makes it, or buy smuggled name-brand merchandise from someone with connections. The homemade variety is the least expensive and involves the least risk. The smuggled-in variety costs $100 a bottle and up.

The do-it-yourselfers seem to be most prevalent at ARAMCO. Through AMS (ARAMCO Material Supplies), those with signature authority can obtain all the stainless steel hardware, monitoring instrumentation and controls necessary to fabricate an automated still. Their automated stills are capable of producing a commercial-grade product. Were not talking Kentucky moonshine here; were talking high-tech, high-quality, low-volume commercial production. Yes, we're even talking Oak-barrel aging.

Sadiki, as the Aramcons call it, is sold as White or Brown. Sadiki is an Arabic word for friend. White comes from the still as pure grain alcohol. It is then cut with distilled water down to 50 to 80 proof. Brown is essentially White that has been aged with Oak. Brown is a smoother drink. I am not a drinker, but I am told that it compares favorably with name-brand Kentucky Bourbon. It looks and smells the same to me, anyway.

Usually, whoever owns a still only distributes within his own circle of friends. By keeping their operation small, the still owner is not likely to be arrested. However, when some are willing to pay $80 per liter for cut-down White, greed sometimes prevails. Some guys make bigger stills and develop black-market outlets for their product. One still-owner that I heard of was caught and sentenced to life in a Saudi prison. The life sentence was because of the size of his business. The man was supposedly bringing in over $5,000 per week. Do it on a small scale and don't get caught appears to be the unofficial ARAMCO policy. Officially, employees can be terminated and deported if caught.

The people that smuggle the genuine article into the country operate with such low visibility that they are known to only a select few. These entrepreneurs know the system and are well connected. The few who are occasionally caught are given either a life sentence or are executed. Because the stakes are so high, the rewards are also high. A Saudi truck driver will start in Jordan with a brand new Mercedes dump truck loaded with quality booze. The black-market value of the booze is around $800,000. The cost of the merchandise is around $50,000. The truck cost is around $150,000. If he makes it to his drop point in Saudi Arabia, he gets to keep the truck. There are a lot of paid-for Mercedes dump trucks in Saudi Arabia.

Being a nondrinker, I had no reason to acquire a source for liquor. However, one of my friends was involved in distributing White. My friend had a wife who was involved with another guy. Since we lived in a small community, my friend knew what was going on and who was doing his wife. The guy happened to be one of his customers. When the guy showed up to purchase White for a big party, my friend sold him uncut pure Sadiki. The uncut Sadiki had an alcohol content four times higher than the standard White. When the unsuspecting buyer hosted a big party, he and many of his guests ended up in the hospital with alcohol poisoning. Everyone that went to the hospital received a one-way ticket home. My friend got rid of his immediate adversary but was still not able to keep his wife at home.

Although most of the drinking is done by non-Saudis, there are certainly Saudis who drink. Some Saudis with political power have private well-stocked bars and know how to entertain. Most do their drinking outside of the kingdom. On one British Air flight to New York, I sat across the isle from a rather small Saudi man. On the other side of the Saudi sat a large, rough-looking expatriate—just back from an offshore rig perhaps. The two pretty much ignored each other for the whole flight except at dinnertime.

As luck would have it, pork-chops were being served. Chicken was the other choice, but all the chicken had been served by the time the stewardess reached my two neighbors. Just before the food was served, both the Saudi and the large expatriate ordered a Scotch. When the food arrived, and the Saudi realized he had been served pork, he summoned the stewardess and verbally assaulted her for daring to serve him pork. She apologized and did manage to find one more chicken dinner for him. His oversized neighbor, who had been sitting quietly throughout the noisy outburst, calmly reached over and grabbed the Saudi's Scotch. As he pulled the drink from the stunned Saudi's hand, he told him, "Since you are a good Muslim, you won't be needing this, either." The Saudi sat quietly and ate his chicken as his neighbor drank both drinks.

The most popular place for Saudis who want to drink is Bahrain. This tiny Island is an independent country. Even before the 26-kilometer causeway was built connecting it with Saudi Arabia, it was just a cheap 15-minute flight away. The cost to fly there was less than the cost of a bottle of smuggled whiskey. Saudis who go to Bahrain to drink do so without risk—that is—as long as they manage to become sober before returning to their own country. Saudi customs agents have sent more than a few citizens to the calaboose for arriving in Dhahran with alcohol on their breath.

For those unwilling to pay for black-market booze, there is always homemade wine or beer. Products already containing alcohol, such as vanilla extract, cough syrup and mouthwash, are also illegal in Saudi Arabia. All the necessary ingredients to make wine or beer, though, are available at every local grocery store. Fortunately for the drinkers, sugar, bottled water, fruit juices, yeast and grains are all staples that would be hard to ban. From what my drinking friends tell me, the local ingredients are good enough to make wine comparable to low-grade commercial wine.

I was afraid to try even the homemade stuff while in Saudi. While in Kuwait, however, I did sample some homemade wine. I was impressed enough to obtain the following Kuwaiti expatriate wine-making instructions:

HOW TO MAKE GOOD WINE IN KUWAIT:

Go to the local suik and purchase two 20-liter plastic Jerry cans. Also purchase about four meters of ¼" or 5 mm clear vinyl tubing. Be sure you have a drill slightly smaller than the tubing size. You will have no trouble at all finding these materials as they are sold at several shops and are always stocked in large quantities. Then, from the local Safeway® or other local supermarket, purchase a case of bottled drinking water (Sohat® is the best), three cases of pure red grape juice (the 1.5-liter bottles with the clampdown ceramic top), two kilos of sugar and a package of baker's yeast. Take all these things home and find a cool, dark hiding place. For best results, the hiding place should have a stable temperature of between 72° F and 76° F.

Be sure to wash the new Jerry cans several times with soap and hot water. Rinse them at least three times with hot water to get all the soap out, and let them dry upside down before using. If you don't start out with clean containers, you will end up with some weird-tasting wine. It will still be drinkable, but you won't be bragging about it to your friends.

Drill a hole in the center of the screw-on cap of one of the plastic Jerry cans. Cut the vinyl tubing into two lengths of about two meters each. Set one aside to use later as a siphon. Insert one end of the tubing through the hole until the inserted end is about two inches inside the container. Do not insert it too far or the gas pressure from the fermenting yeast will force some of your wine out through the tube. Later on, you will stick the free end of the tube into a bottle of water. This will act as a gas trap that will let the carbon dioxide from the fermenting yeast escape but will prevent oxygen from entering. If you don't put the tube in water, you will make vinegar instead of wine. If you don't use a gas trap at all and just screw on the lid, you will make a bomb capable of blowing your closet door well into the living room.

Fill a one-liter jar about one-third full of lukewarm bottled drinking water. Add about one-half-cup of sugar. Add a package of yeast and stir until everything is dissolved. Place the jar in the center of a large baking dish inside your cupboard. Within three or four hours, the fermenting yeast will be foaming out of the jar and into the baking dish. If the yeast doesn't foam up, either the water is too cold or the yeast is dead. If it doesn't foam, do this step over until you have an active yeast culture.

Pour ten 1.5-liter bottles of red grape juice into one container. In a large open pot or bowl, dissolve two kilos of sugar into three liters of Sohat® drinking water. Pour the water and sugar mix into the container. Dump the active yeast mix into the container. Screw the lid with the tubing on tightly and shake the container around a bit. Place the container on a chair or on a stand in your hiding place. When it comes time to siphon, you will be happier if the bottom of the container is resting two or three feet above your bottles. Place the free end of the tubing in a half-full bottle of water with the tubing inserted all the way to the bottom of the water bottle. Close the door.

Three to four weeks later, open the door and check on your project. First, check to be sure the gas-trap bottle is not still bubbling. A bubble every few minutes is OK; a bubble every few seconds means it is still actively fermenting. Use a flashlight to look inside the container to be sure the liquid is translucent. If these two tests are passed, it's time to siphon to the second container. If not, put everything back together and wait another week. Do not disturb the primary container. The slightest movement will stir-up bottom residue. Bottom residue tastes as bad as it looks—and it looks nasty.

Insert one end of the clean siphon tube (the other piece of vinyl tubing) into the liquid. The end of the tubing should be no closer to the bottom than 2". It helps to put a mark of some kind on your siphon to indicate the absolute lowest level of insertion. The bottom 1" of liquid, which is mostly yeast sludge, should be discarded. If you must bottle the last liter, save it for those guests that show up for dinner uninvited.

Siphon all but the bottom 2" of liquid into a clean container. You can bottle directly at this point, but you will be violating Paul's rule of "No wine before its time." Place the newly filled second container on the chair or stand, connect the gas trap as was done previously, and let it finish for another three to four weeks. This time, bottle all but the bottom inch. Put about a cup of pure white grape juice in the bottom of each bottle before bottling. This will lower the net alcohol level to about 12% and will mellow the wine. Place the bottled wine in a wine rack and store it for at least three months before drinking (Paul's rule again).

The finished product will be a translucent pale red wine. If aged long enough, the taste will be smooth and fruity. With practice, and experimentation, you can make wines worth bragging about. If you are making your wine in Kuwait, brag quietly. If you are making your wine in Saudi Arabia, brag silently.

Killer Camels From Kuwait

Traffic on The Way to The Airport

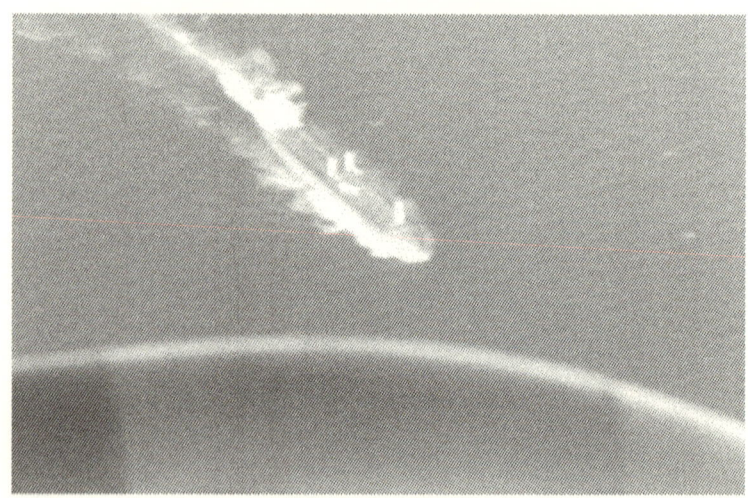

Approaching Dhahran

AIRPORTS

The only practical way to get to Saudi Arabia is by air. No ocean liner calls at any Saudi port, and there are no intercontinental railway connections. You could drive or walk in, but you'd have to be pretty adventurous. To get there from Europe, you would have to pass through Bosnia, Turkey and Iraq. To get there from Asia, you would have to pass through Iran and Iraq. To get there from Africa, you'd have to part the Red Sea. (That hasn't been done for a while.)

The airport at Dhahran services all of ARAMCO and most of the Eastern Province of Saudi Arabia.

The airport at Riyadh services Riyadh and the Royals. Because of the Royals, the Riyadh airport was probably the most expensive airport in the world to construct—and is probably the most beautiful. It is an architectural monument to egocentric opulence.

The airport at Jeddah services all of the Western Province—including Mecca. With several million people using the airport during the two-week Hajj season, it is by necessity the largest airport in the world. All three of the Saudi international airports share the same advantages and the same problems.

The new airports are quite a contrast to the undersized, run-down, overcrowded, outdated airport where I first landed in 1977. That old Dhahran Airport was mass confusion twenty-four hours per day. During Hajj, when several million Muslims passed through in a two-week period, it was ten-guys-in-a-Volkswagen times several-hundred-thousand. Ironically, in spite of the crowds and confusion, on a normal day it was faster to pass through the old airport than it is now to pass through any of the newer airports. Though the confused and fragrant masses where in a perpetual state of chaos, it was physically only a short distance from the entrance to the boarding ramp. At any time but Hajj and Ramadan, a person could pass through the old

Dhahran airport in less than ninety minutes—and most of that time was spent checking in.

The new airports at Dhahran, Riyadh and Jeddah were designed to be everything the old airports were not. The new airports are efficient, beautiful, high-tech, clean, orderly and immense. Every aspect of each new airport is built on a massive scale. It now takes at least three hours to get through any one of them.

In their quest to have the biggest and the best, the Saudis went a bit overboard. Construction costs for the world's three largest airports would put a serious dent in our national debt. The largest airport, on the edge of Jeddah, covers over fifty square miles. Besides having numerous runways capable of handling supersonic aircraft, the Jeddah airport has five separate terminals that are really stand-alone airports unto themselves. They each have their own entrances and exits, and they each cater to a specific group of patrons.

The two main terminals are conventional domestic and international airports. They are similar in size to LAX or Dallas. Though they function quite smoothly under heavy loads, their shear size makes them a nightmare for travelers. From the center of Jeddah, it is a half-hour drive just to reach the freeway. From the nearest freeway airport exit, it is another half-hour trip just to the ticket counter. Parking is similar to LAX parking.

The Disney-style serpentine ticket lines at the new airport are much nicer than the old mass-mob-at-the-window scenario of days gone by. At the old airport, whoever was able to stick their fist-full-of-money farthest into the ticket window bought their ticket next. Pushing and shoving was OK; profanity would get you arrested. In both scenarios, the wait for a ticket is about 45 minutes, but the new method is less stressful.

Ticketed travelers, after checking their baggage, pass through security and passport control. Assuming one's exit visa is valid, this procedure adds an additional half-hour to the process. It's a little faster in the domestic terminal because there is no passport stamping involved.

The primary problem at each new airport is geography. With the ends of some runways as much as ten miles from the terminal, it is not practical to taxi planes to the gates. Instead, special oversized busses were built to transport passengers from the gate to the plane. These busses are built on hydraulic scissor frames that allow them to rise up to the gate or up to the plane for loading and unloading. During transport, the bus body is lowered for safety. Technically, the system works well.

The down side of the high-tech system is time. The bus ride adds 30 to 45 minutes to the process. Passengers catching a plane that leaves at Midnight, must board the bus at the gate at 10:45 PM. At 11:00 PM, the bus heads for the plane. Considering the time-consuming process of catching a plane out of Jeddah, a passenger on the midnight flight must arrive at the airport no later than 9 PM. If a passenger starts from the side of Jeddah farthest from the airport, it can be a 5-hour process from the office to the plane.

The Hajj terminal is used exclusively by people performing the Hajj. All Muslims who are able to do so are obliged to make at least one holy pilgrimage to Mecca in their lifetime. Those who can afford it come every year. There is a specific two-week holiday-period set aside every year just for this purpose. The holiday is called Hajj, and all those who participate are called Hajjis. The lunar month that the holiday falls in is also called Hajj. There are several million Hajjis each year. For business travelers, Hajj is the worst time to enter or leave the country. Before the new airport, it was nearly impossible to get into or out of Jeddah during Hajj. To mitigate such nightmares, the new airport was designed with a special Hajj terminal.

The Hajj terminal is completely isolated from the other four terminals. Over ninety percent of its visitors arrive only during Hajj. By necessity, it is a city unto itself. It includes an immense staging area for sleeping over and for catching government-run shuttle busses to Mecca. The freestanding structures shading the staging area are as tall as a high-rise office building. The complex is considered to be the world's largest tent. Its glaring white reflective surfaces are made of high-tech fibers developed by Dow-Corning®. The multiple-tent-shaped structures can be seen from more than twenty miles away. Every aspect of the main terminal, including customs, is duplicated at the Hajj terminal. It is the international doorway to Mecca. Only Muslims are allowed to use it.

The fourth terminal is exclusively for the Royals. I cannot personally describe the inside of this monolithic wonder. It is quite impressive on the outside. This terminal has a short, guarded access drive, has the most impressive landscaping, has no ticket counter or customs to worry about, and the private 747's and Lear jets pull right up to the gate. The King doesn't like long lines.

A friend who worked on building the terminal told me it is all fresh flowers, hand-woven carpets, marble columns and ornate artwork inside. It is literally another royal palace. The weekly changing of thousands of potted, blooming flowers keeps a crew of gardeners busy full-time. Because of security risks, each gardener and each pot is inspected before being allowed entry into the terminal. The average lottery winner could not afford even the gardeners.

The greenhouse and nursery complex that supplies the flowers is located on Airport property. The greenhouses may be the most elaborate high-tech greenhouses in the world. The nursery complex is built on a piece of land the size of a championship golf course. The triple-glazed glass houses have computer-controlled shade, humidity, light and temperature. Flowering plants from all corners of the world are grown and made to bloom out of season. The greenhouses alone cost over $20 million to construct. Annual operating costs for the nursery are in the millions. The complex is a high-volume, high-quality flower factory built and operated just to keep the airport colorful.

The last terminal is not really a terminal—it is a military post. All airports in Saudi Arabia are also used by the military. The security for military installations is extreme. Anyone attempting to photograph any part of a Saudi airport risks being arrested as a spy. At the very least, such an indiscretion will cost a person a camera and some uncomfortable time in an interrogation room. When near these areas, paranoia is a prudent partner to common sense. Spies are shot.

Critics of the new airports cite the shorter pass-through time of the old airports. The argument is that smaller and less complicated equals cheaper, better and faster. (Perhaps the critics should talk to NASA.) These distracters fail to remember the total entropy associated with the older airports. The departure lounge was standing room only. It was hot, smelly, noisy and poorly lit. Part of the reason people made it through faster was that it was too stressful to linger. People just braced themselves and pushed through the crowd. Planes were never on schedule. Occasionally, they departed early causing people who were on time and with tickets to miss the plane. Baggage was lost or damaged, and overworked airport employees were always a bit testy.

The new airports, on the other hand, are spacious, airy, well lit, well organized and comfortable. The one design problem that I noticed was with the signs on the hamams (rest rooms). When they put the standard stickman icons on the doors, the old Saudi men misunderstood the symbols. To them, the stick man represented Western people who wear pants. The stick woman represented Saudi men who wear a dress-like garment called a thobe. I understood the problem the first time I saw a red-faced old Saudi man come hurrying out of the lady's rest room. The airport staff figured it out, too. The next time I passed through, the sign on the men's room had a profile of a man with a beard and the sign on the lady's room had a profile of a woman with a veil.

Overall, the planners of these man-made wonders did well. It is easy to complain about how long it takes to pass through such huge airports, but the experience is pleasant. The huge sky-lit common areas with fountains and ever-blooming flowers are quite uplifting. These are the largest, most beautiful airports in the world. They handle an incredible volume of passengers.

People get the luggage they started out with. The planes leave on time and arrive on time. The only legitimate complaint—the three-hour pass-through time—is an unavoidable byproduct of volume and size. Perhaps the critics should try the land route.

Killer Camels From Kuwait

Donkey Cart with 15-inch Chevy Wheels

My First Company Car in Dhahran

FROM A DONKEY TO A MERCEDES BENZ

In 1974, when the Arab countries held the world hostage over oil, money started flowing into Saudi Arabia. With money came automobiles—not just for the rich—for everyone. In one year, the entire country went from a donkey or camel to a Toyota or Mercedes Benz. Never mind that there were no good roads or that no one knew how to drive, everyone bought a car. At one point, shortly after the oil embargo, the annual Saudi death rate from automobile accidents exceeded the Saudi birth rate.

By the time I arrived in 1977, a few good roads had been built and many more were under construction. Everyone had a car, and everyone was learning to drive by trial and error. At ARAMCO, we were not allowed to drive until we had completed a put-the-fear-of-God-in-you defensive driving course. Even then, we were encouraged to avoid driving after dark.

After completing the course, I was issued a small Datsun 180B. I quickly realized that my chance of surviving even a minor crash in such a small car was low. Most of the locals were driving big American or German cars. Within a month, I convinced my department head to give me a more practical vehicle. I was assigned a one-ton crew-cab GMC pickup with a pipe rack, wench, and extra-heavy steel bumpers. The idea was to be large, visible, and intimidating.

In 1978, the Saudi government built their first overpass on a new freeway near ARAMCO headquarters in Dhahran. It was a beautiful bridge with almost twenty feet of clearance between the road below and the bottom of the bridge. It was the first time in Arabia that anything of substance had been suspended above a roadway. Within a week of the bridge being opened, a Mercedes flatbed truck, with an oversized piece of heavy machinery, drove under the bridge. The machinery struck the bridge and took out one entire side of the bridge. It was speculated that the truck was traveling in excess of 90 MPH when it went under the bridge.

The bridge had to be torn down, redesigned, and rebuilt a little higher.

In the Western Province (where the oil wasn't), freeway construction started much later. Before the freeway was built between Jeddah and Yanbu, there was a two-lane road that connected the two cities. The road was about 200 miles long. I traveled that road many times both day and night. Whenever a new guy came on board, I would always make a bet with him. I would tell him that if we could stop at any point along the road to Yanbu and not see a wrecked vehicle in either direction, I would give him one hundred dollars. I would let him tell me when to stop. I never lost that bet.

In the several years that I drove that rode, I personally witnessed numerous fatal crashes. The worst head-on wrecks always involved Mercedes dump trucks or fully loaded passenger busses. The road was relatively straight but had a lot of rises and dips that hid oncoming headlights from view—hidden, that is, until you were passing and it was too late to react. One night, while hurrying to meet a plane, I experienced exactly such a situation. There must have been angels coordinating the event. I passed a truck at night and didn't realize the highway had a slight rise to it. As I crested the hill, I found myself almost grill-to-grill with an oncoming bus. Just as I was about to become a landmark, the Mercedes dump truck to my right moved over. Simultaneously, I straddled the centerline—almost touching the truck. The oncoming bus veered onto the shoulder. All of us were exceeding 80 MPH. In less than the blink of an eye, the oncoming bus that surely would have killed me was in my rear view mirror. I slowed down, pulled to the side of the road, shook, prayed, and decided meeting the plane on time was unimportant—better to meet the new guy later than not at all.

I once stopped to photograph one of those mass-death wrecks. The police and rescue squads had just left with the living and the dead. I figured a photo of the grisly scene was necessary for all the folks back home who had difficulty believing my stories. Leaving my car on the roadside, camera in hand, I walked over to a bus that had tried to morph with a loaded Mercedes dump truck. Both vehicles were about 50% shorter than they had been before the crash. The bus appeared to be turned almost inside out. When I got close enough to take a good photo, I started seeing details that were not visible from the road. The rescue squad people had only taken the larger pieces with them. Blood was everywhere, and there were still body parts enmeshed within the jagged metal wreckage. I did not take a photo. I got back into my car, said the necessary prayers, and did not think about that scene again until after I had left the country. I could not have continued driving there if I had allowed that image to linger.

In the mid 1980s, the freeway to Yanbu was completed. I am sure it has saved at least three or four thousand lives each year since it was built. However, when it first opened, it was something new, and the local drivers did not know how to use it. The first week it was open, I drove by two Mercedes dump trucks that had hit head-on in the southbound lane. It had been foggy the night before, and one of the drivers had entered on an off ramp. They must have both felt safe driving in the fog at high speed knowing that there would be no oncoming traffic. Both trucks were fully loaded with rock. The trucks hit so hard that the dump boxes of each truck ended up touching each other. The three feet or so of compacted metal between the two dump boxes was all that was left of the driver compartments. Clearly, it was not possible to extract the drivers from such a wreck.

A little farther down the road, a Chevy Suburban was coming straight at me. The man was driving slowly, was flashing his lights and honking his horn. When he drove by me, he yelled "Kisumic Sharmuta." I will not translate his greeting. At the time, I found it quite humorous that some people would not understand which side of the freeway they should be on.

A week later, shortly after dusk, a similar event happened. This time, though, it happened at a slight rise in the road. There was a guy behind me who had decided to pass about the same time a wrong-way driver came my way. We were all doing at least 70 MPH. I heard a tremendous WUMP just about where my left-side blind spot was. The wind-force from the crash pushed the rear of my car slightly to the right. I nearly lost control trying to compensate for the directional shift. I thought about the non-serious incident from the week before. It was no longer funny.

About the only funny thing that ever happened to me while driving in Arabia was an incident involving a train near the ARAMCO facilities at Abqaiq. There is only one train operating in Saudi Arabia; it runs from Dammam to Riyadh. There was once another train in the western province, but Lawrence of Arabia blew it up. What's left of that train is rusting in the desert northwest of Yanbu.

The problem with having only one train in the country is that crossing a railroad track is a rare occurrence for most motorists. I was quite amazed one day when I saw an outdated passenger train slowly making its way across the road in front of me. By the time I arrived at the crossing, there were four or five trucks in front of me. It was a long train and more trucks and cars arrived. In about a ten-minute period, about 50 or 60 vehicles had arrived. Since everyone wanted to see the train as closely as possible, the cars lined up about eight-across on what was a two-lane road: four on one side of the white line and four on the other side of the white line. It took about ten minutes for the train to pass.

As the last train car passed the intersection, I put my car in gear and prepared to move on. Unfortunately, none of us could go anywhere. While we were all busy lining up on the west side of the train, an equally large number of vehicles had lined up on the east side of the train. We found ourselves facing one another like two football teams. Fortunately, no one yelled, "Hike." It took over four hours of horn-honking and imaginative epitaphs to get everyone across the track. After that, I made a point of checking the train schedule before driving to Abqaiq.

In the late 1970s or early 1980s, the local police in Dhahran decided to purchase police motorcycles. They bought a large number of Kawasaki KZ-1000's. The Saudi policemen assigned to ride those rockets barely knew how to ride bicycles. The taller officers were about five-feet tall and weighed in under 110 lb. For those who don't know, the KZ-1000 is faster off the line than a Corvette or a Porsche. These are the same bikes that much larger experienced policemen ride on American highways.

The first week the bikes were on the streets, you saw them everywhere. Those little guys were having a ball harassing the local motorists. I noticed two motorcycles that had been smashed pretty badly that first week, but, in general, they quickly learned to ride and actually demonstrated great skill at surviving the rush-hour traffic flow. The bikes probably would have worked well for them if it had not been for the sand.

Saudi Sand is not like beach sand. Saudi sand, which was formed by wind instead of by water, does not have the fractured edges of beach sand. Saudi sand has a rounded surface. It is less like tiny rocks and more like tiny ball bearings. It is powder-fine sand that doesn't hurt much when it blows into your eyes. Often the roads in Saudi Arabia become covered with a fine layer of this sandy dust.

On windy days, when there was lots of powdery sand blowing around, there always seemed to be more car accidents. As car accidents occurred, motorcycle cops were dispatched to take care of things. In the course of getting from the station to the accident scene, there were corners and curves to negotiate. The more sand there was on the road, the less often the Saudi policeman made it around the corner. It took less than one year for nearly every police bike in service to crash. Several policemen were killed. For a while after the last police bike disappeared from the Saudi streets, the local police considered motorcycles to be illegal vehicles in Dhahran. Whenever the police found someone with a motorcycle, they confiscated it and added it to a growing pile of motorcycles at the police station in Dammam. After several months, they poured fuel on the pile and torched the bikes. I saw the huge pile but could only speculate as to how many of those police bikes were at the bottom.

To help you understand what driving is really like in Saudi Arabia, I will share the view from behind the wheel. A typical drive from your office in Dhahran to your apartment in Al Khobar goes something like this:

The drive from the office to the main gate is more or less like driving in your own neighborhood. Immediately outside the gate, though, you enter another world. Every car has a horn, and every driver uses his horn with great gusto. Some honk to warn others to get out of their way. Others, I am convinced, honk simply because they believed it makes their car go faster. No matter the reason, the din of thousands of horns blaring from all sides is quite distracting. Within a month, though, you learn to tune it out. A good amplified stereo system helps.

Besides the noise, the first thing you notice outside the ARMCO gate is the shear speed at which everyone is driving. On a road that might be safe at 30 MPH, everyone is driving at 70 MPH. A few cars are weaving in and out of the lanes at even faster speeds. The whole scene is reminiscent of a stock car race. The speeds are about the same. The cars are about as beat up. Each driver is trying to take the lead. The only two unsettling differences are that the crashes are much bloodier and that you are in the race. At full throttle, you insert your vehicle into the stream of traffic.

The road is designed to be a four-lane road: two lanes on each side with a divider in the middle. There is a wide soft shoulder and at least 30 feet of semi-compacted sand on either side of the road. A good 50 feet from the edge of the soft shoulder, there are steel light poles about 150 feet apart. It is actually a well-designed road with good lighting and a planter-box median that may someday be landscaped.

Somehow, the drivers today have decided that this road actually has 3 1/2 to 4 lanes on each side. It is difficult to tell exactly how many lanes there are at any one time because no one is exactly behind or in front of anyone else. Each driver is trying to get around every other driver and is jockeying for a position that will allow him to pass at the next opportunity.

The drivers on the outside lanes have the advantage because they can swerve out into the desert to get around. At the speed everyone is going, the semi-compacted sand does not stop anyone from completing such a maneuver. However, the regularly-spaced light poles do.

The light poles were part of a state-of-the-art street lighting system installed by a French contractor. The poles were installed far enough from the road that they should have been safe from the most reckless motorist. On this particular road, though, every single pole has been struck at least once. Some of the poles have been hit so strongly that they now lean out toward the desert or in toward the street. Incredibly, all are still working. About every fifth pole still has a Datsun or Toyota stuck to it. It's amazing how each crashed car has somehow managed to hit its respective pole dead center in the middle of the grill.

In the time it took you to read about this, you have traveled a good three miles from the ARAMCO gate. There is a series of speed bumps near the Petroleum University. The bumps were put there to allow students to cross the road. Of course, the University students are too smart to attempt such a feat. No one slows for the speed bumps. Actually, everyone speeds up. Everyone has learned that the bumps are only a problem if hit at any speed below 60 MPH. Taken at any higher speed, they have almost no effect. The rusting speed limit sign at the crossing reads 20 KPH in Arabic (about 12 MPH).

Three more miles and you come to the first stoplight. The light has been red for several seconds so some of the cars try to stop—or at least slow down. Miraculously, you are able to stop at the front of the pack and no one hits you from behind. As you wait for the light to change, everyone lays on their horns. Not to be left out, you do the same. As you sit there, you notice that the road has become six or seven lanes wide. The lane to the far left is halfway onto the median. The three right lanes are all off the

111

pavement. You look across the intersection and notice that the road ahead has two lanes with high curbs on each side and light poles that are next to the curbs.

The light changes and you floor it. Several cars beat you through the funnel. You know better than to look to either side. If another driver catches your glance, he assumes you are giving him the right-of-way. As you enter the real right lane on the other side, you hear a muted thud to your right. The car on your right has just hit the curb and bounced in just behind you.

Everyone's speed has dropped to a safer 40 MPH. In your GMC truck from hell, you are confident that you could survive any crash at this speed. You stop at the next red light and feel a slight bump at your rear. You ignore it—to do otherwise would be to risk going to jail. You notice that the man on your left has his right blinker on. You wrongly assume that he just forgot to turn it off. When the light turns green, both you and your neighbor floor it. Even though you are doing almost the same speed, he cuts his vehicle hard right forcing you to slam on the brakes. He makes his right turn and the car behind you bumps you a little harder and honks. You both keep going.

Two more intersections and you arrive in front of your apartment. You park off-street in the vacant lot next door. Your roommate made the mistake of parking on the street the week before and came out in the morning to find his car to be about 2 inches narrower than it had been when he parked it. It's now time to get some rest and prepare for the drive back to the office the next morning.

That was how it was in the '70s and '80s. In fairness to the Saudis, though, a little perspective is in order: Our grandfather's learned to drive when there were few cars and slow cars. Our parents learned from their parents on roads with a few more cars and somewhat faster cars. By the time we learned how to drive, we had ridden thousands of miles with our parents and grandparents. We already knew the rules of the road and had firsthand experience at riding in vehicles that cruise at over 70 MPH. The Saudis, on the other hand, went straight from the donkey to the Mercedes. They went from 3 MPH to 100 MPH in one step. They paid cash for their first car, and the salesman showed them how to start it and how to work the gearshift. They figured out how to use the brake as they drove—or not. It was trial and error on a national scale. Everyone started driving at the same time with no one to show the way. We who make fun of them would have done no better under the same circumstance. To this day, some Arabs still believe that the whole mess was a CIA plot.

Over a nine-year period, I experienced many adventures on the roads of Saudi Arabia and Kuwait. During that period, in-kingdom auto accidents killed nearly a dozen of my friends. I had two friends crushed by Mercedes dump trucks. I had a friend killed when his car struck a camel on a foggy night. I lost several friends to head-on accidents—some on the freeway. A few friends were killed in broadside crashes, and one acquaintance bled to death at the scene of a relatively minor accident because the police would not let the rescue squad people take him until a report was finished.

When I left the Middle East, in 1986, the roads had come up to par with roads in America. The drivers had learned how to drive and survive, and the death rate from auto accidents, while still staggering, was nowhere near the country's birth rate. With another decade or so of practice, they may all become quite good drivers. Perhaps then it will be safe enough to let their women drive.

Coral in The Red Sea

Looking for Red Grouper

Reef Eaters (pretty but not tasty)

THE RED SEA

God Parted the Red Sea to help Moses and the Israelites elude Pharaoh's army. For Moses, the Red Sea was just an obstacle on the way to the Promised Land. For SCUBA divers, the Red Sea is the Promised Land.

The barren landscape on either shore offers no clue to what exists below. The landscape is rock, sand and sparse vegetation. The surface of the sea appears as varying shades of turquoise and blue. The seascape below, however, is a pristine coral reef populated with abundant marine life.

The water is never cold. Even in January, the water temperature does not get below about 70° F. In August, water temperatures will be above 85° F. Much to the delight of divers, water temperatures do not drop much as you descend. Summer diving to depths of forty feet does not require a wet suit. In these tropical waters, wet suits are worn not for warmth but for protection against solar radiation and fire coral. A sweatshirt, jeans and old tennis shoes will work, too.

Upon entering the water, divers new to the Red Sea are surprised by the visibility. The water is even clearer than it appears from the surface. On a good day, visibility is over two hundred feet. On a really bad day, it will be down to seventy-five feet. The water is so clear that it startles some first-timers.

An engineer who snorkeled for the first time near Yanbu was so terrified when he passed over a deep chasm that he turned and clung to an outcropping coral head. I motioned for him to follow me, but he just hung there shaking his head. Actually, his whole body was shaking. He told me later that even though he is a good swimmer, looking down into the abyss was too much for him. In his mind, as clear as the water was, it was like stepping off the roof of a ten-story building. Even though logic told him he would just float on the surface, being able to see clearly all the way to the bottom of a hundred-foot-deep chasm was just too overwhelming.

Levitating over, down and through an undersea panorama of coral columns, cliffs and caves causes a euphoric sense of being that is quite addictive. Levitation is the most appropriate description for the sensation. Nowhere else have I felt so unfettered below the surface.

Starting from shore, in the shallow water before the actual reef, the bottom is a mixture of sand, small coral heads and sea grass. In this microenvironment, there are many small fish, sea cucumbers and mollusks. For anyone afraid of the deeper water and the larger creatures, this shallow pre-reef area offers many safe adventures. Although the fish are small and the coral heads are miniature, everything is brightly colored, constantly in motion and fascinating to watch. Its very much like snorkeling in a large, overstocked aquarium.

On the seaward side of the reef, the sea floor rises up to meet the first ridge of coral. This coral barrier lies just inches below the surface during the lowest tides of the month. At high tide, when the swells are mild, a diver or a small boat can safely glide over the ridge. Crossing the reef at low tide cannot be done with a boat and can only be done by a diver with adequate body protection. Although resembling a giant bouquet of cauliflower or broccoli, coral has more in common with a giant bouquet of razor blades.

Once across the ridge, the seascape changes. In the shallow pre-reef area, man is a giant invader. On the seaward side of the reef, man is a puny alien. The sudden change of scale makes this a real-life Gulliver adventure. Pre-reef barrel-sized corals give way to coral heads the size of houses. Huge schools of large fish glide in and out of view. A silvery school of Barracuda flashes by like an explosion. A shadow passing overhead turns out to be a giant Manta Ray with a wingspan of nearly twenty feet. The entrance to a coral cave is blocked by a two-foot-wide Red Grouper. A Sea Turtle gracefully glides by about two hundred feet away—just at the edge of what's visible.

Ascending to the top of the coral heads, there are brightly colored fish with lots of white, yellow, orange, brilliant blue and neon green. Descending back down through the overbearing coral columns and delicate fan-shaped outcroppings, everything becomes green, blue, gray and black. At seventy feet, the bottom is covered with slipper coral, starfish, giant clams and various bottom-dwelling creatures. Some of the giant clams are as large as a car engine. An underwater light reveals colors just as bright as those near the surface. With the light off, though, the seascape is a serene grayish-blue-green.

From the base of the shallow barrier ridge, the reef extends seaward for several hundred feet. Looking back toward shore, it becomes clear that the shallow coral ridge is actually the top of a coral cliff. These coral cliffs measure anywhere from thirty feet tall to over one hundred feet tall. The sea floor then slopes gently to a deeper ridge which is anywhere from eighty feet to one hundred feet below the surface. From the deep ridge, the floor drops at an incredibly steep angle to depths of over one thousand feet.

Looking over the edge of the deep ridge is like looking into the deepest black hole you can imagine. Even experienced divers instinctively reel from the sight of the dark abyss. Just before reaching the deep ridge, there is a major thermal barrier. The drastic drop in water temperature adds to one's sense of foreboding. Thoughts of exploring the deeper depths bring to mind the nightmares of nitrogen narcosis, oxygen toxia and the bends. Added to these medical risks of diving deep are the large deep-water denizens that frequently appear from out of the black lower depths. There are over three hundred species of sharks in the Red Sea—including the Great White.

Unfortunately, the big sharks are not restricted to only the deeper waters. At one popular diving spot, near a Saudi Coast Guard station, there was a large, rubber channel-marker buoy. The buoy was anchored to the edge of the reef in about thirty feet of water. The water in the channel was about one hundred feet deep. We normally snorkeled on the reef near the buoy. One day several of us showed up to do some snorkeling and noticed that the buoy was missing. We snorkeled down to where it had been anchored and found the buoy—or what was left of it. The six-foot-high buoy was made of inch-thick rubber. It had been bitten in half. From the size of the bite, we decided it was the work of a large Great White Shark. We stopped diving there.

About sixty miles north of Yanbu, we found a better place to dive. It wasn't because the reef was more pristine and had more interesting corals. It wasn't because it was more remote and secluded (although that had a little to do with it). It was because of the other beach patrons who frequented that particular beach. That beach, we discovered, turned out to be the favorite beach of the Swedish nurses and doctors who were assigned to the Yanbu Medical Center.

When we first discovered the beach, we arrived before the Swedish group. We were drawn to the area because it had a good sandy entry point. Once in the water, we found it had even more to offer. There was a narrow breach in the coral ridge that allowed safe passage to the outer reef at low tide. While we were exploring the outer reef, the Swedish group arrived and took over the beach area.

Later that day, as we passed back through the break in the reef and into the shallow water, we noticed several people swimming near the shore. As we snorkeled closer, we noticed that half of the swimmers were female. A bit closer and we noticed that all of them were nude. Losing your snorkel and choking on salt water makes for a dandy first impression.

After clearing our snorkels, we slowly snorkeled on past the swimmers and walked to our vehicles. One of the guys in our group walked back to the beach to talk to the swimmers. There were six beautiful blond Swedish nurses and six blond, rather ordinary, Swedish doctors (six married couples it turned out). They came to this particular beach every weekend because it was remote enough for them to swim nude without being arrested.

We saw them there several times after that. We were careful not to gawk too much, and we pretended to ignore them. We never joined them for fear that they wouldn't come back. We all swore to secrecy and never told any of our other friends about our secret little beach. We had discovered the real Swedish Bikini Team—and they didn't wear bikinis.

A few hundred miles south of Secret Beach is the Sharm at Jeddah. Things are a bit different at the public beach. Here, Saudi families picnic and play games in the sand. Although most Saudis do not actually swim, many do like to wade into the warm water. Their moral code, however, does not allow them to wear just a bathing suit, so they go into the sea with all their clothes on. It is common to see Saudi women with full habias and veils submerged up to their necks.

Only the foreigners wear bathing suits. Foreign women usually wear one-piece conservative bathing suits covered over with a T-shirt or sweatshirt. Bikinis are out of the question for even the boldest female expatriate. Such outrageous behavior will result in arrest and deportation. Anyway, there are plenty of other good reasons for wearing your clothes when going into the Red Sea.

On one occasion, while snorkeling with only shorts and a T-shirt, I scraped my leg on the coral ridge. Immediately on the other side of the ridge, the coral dropped straight down to a depth of about sixty feet. I descended straight down the cliff-face to a depth of about thirty or forty feet. I felt an itch on my thigh and stopped. As I touched the itchy place, it stung. I looked at my leg and saw what appeared to be gray smoke wafting off my leg. Because the longer wavelengths of light do not penetrate very far below the surface, my blood appeared as gray smoke. Not wanting to attract the White-tipped Reef Shark I saw meandering my way, I called it a day and returned to shore.

As I walked back to my vehicle, blood streamed down my leg and into my tennis shoe. The slash in my thigh could have used stitching, but I was too macho. By the next day, an infection had set in. It required a series of antibiotics and several weeks of limping and wincing to heal the wound.

Some areas of the reef are populated with sea snakes. These three-foot-long snakes have a fin-like tale that allows them to swim quite well. Fortunately, their mouths are so small that they can only bite a human at a fold in the skin, on a finger, or on a toe. Unfortunately for the rare few who are bitten, sea snakes are the most venomous snakes on the planet. They are normally shy but do become quite aggressive during mating season. Throughout the several years I spent diving in the Red Sea and the Arabian Gulf, I only heard of one person, a fisherman, who had been bitten. He died before reaching the hospital.

A more common danger than the sea snake is the Lion Fish. These black and white zebra-striped fish with graceful oversized fins are strikingly beautiful. Their fins, however, have sharp spines with venom less toxic than that of the sea snake but which causes even more pain. Most fishermen and divers know that a prick from the fin of a Lion Fish will ruin a perfectly good day.

On one outing to the beach near Yanbu, I was flagged down by a 4wd pickup full of Filipinos. A man in the back of the truck was wreathing in agony. One of his buddies held up a spear that still had a Lion Fish impaled on its tip.

"He was stung by this fish, sir. What should we do?"

I remember his friend's urgent plea, and to this day, I still feel bad about what I told him. I said, "Oh no. That's a Lion Fish. If you are stung by one of those, you only have a couple of hours to live. Take him to the hospital immediately." I told him that knowing it was almost a two-hour drive to the hospital. I was about to tell him that he might have a little more than two hours, but they took off before I could say any more. There was nothing in the news that evening about a truck accident or about anyone dying from a Lion Fish sting, so I guess he made it. Of course, if the guard at the hospital saw that illegal spear gun, their medical emergency may have been the least of their problems.

The weekend after the Filipino was stung, I had a little dose of bad karma. I knew about Fire Coral but doubted its reputation. I was diving without gloves and came across an incredibly beautiful outcropping of Fire Coral. The formation was fan-shaped and flat. It was structured like a fine filigree gold piece. It was dark orange at the base and gradually faded to lighter orange near the tips. The very tips were ivory in color. It was beautiful. I just reached out and grabbed it.

Wow! Fire Coral has a lot of energy. It felt as if I had grabbed a high-voltage power line. As soon as I let go, my fingers went numb, my forearm began to itch, and my palm felt as if someone were holding a blowtorch to it. It took three weeks for the itching in my forearm to go away. Fire Coral! Of course—what else would you call it?

Let's take stock here: Fire Coral is beautiful, Lion Fish are beautiful, Barracuda are beautiful, jellyfish are beautiful, sharks are beautiful. I think there's a pattern here. The one ugly exception to this pattern is the giant grouper. Discovering that break in the pattern was quite an experience.

Three friends and I were snorkeling off of Secret Beach. The coral terrain there is something like a scaled-down Grand Canyon. Ridges of coral form long, deep, parallel canyons. In some areas, there are holes in the canyon walls that form short caves that pass through to the next canyon. Most of the coral caves are rimmed with outcroppings of Fire Coral.

Feeling euphoric and out for adventure, we dove down and through several of the short caves. Not all caves went all the way through and not all were short. For this reason, we always did a checkout dive before swimming through a new cave. On one such checkout dive, I looked into what appeared to be a dark cave. As I moved in closer to the entrance, a pair of large eyes moved out toward me. I was too high on the moment to rationalize the implication of two large eyes set more than two-feet apart.

I waved my arms to scare it. When I waved my arms, the grouper opened its toothy mouth. My high turned to terror as reality engaged. I found myself facing down a fish large enough to take my head off with one bite. I was invading his private territory and he was defending it. I slowly backed away and drifted toward the surface while continuing to face the big fish. As I drifted up and away from his lair, he followed. With all four of us swimming backwards like big shrimp, the giant grouper followed us for a good one hundred yards. Then he turned, shat a big gray cloud of fish poop, and returned to his den.

There were two humiliating lessons learned that day. The first, of course, was to show a little respect for big fish. The second was realizing that those strange gray clouds we had been swimming through all day were fish poop.

There is actually much more to see in the Red Sea than coral and fish. A man I met by chance in Yanbu had discovered an ancient wreck on the outer reef somewhere near Yanbu. He would never tell me exactly where it was and would never take me diving with him. He did, however, show me some of the artifacts he had hauled up from the wreck. He had boxes and boxes of amber. He had many large urns or vases—the kind with handles on each side and a pointed bottom. I always suspected he had found much more valuable treasure, too, but he never admitted it. I doubt he told the Ministry of Saudi Arabian Antiquities of his discovery.

For months after meeting the guy with the artifacts, several of my friends and I became weekend treasure hunters. We never found a sunken ship, but we did discover some interesting diving areas. The most interesting diving area in the whole Red Sea, though, was not discovered by me or by any of the guys I dove with. It was discovered by a man I met after I returned to the States.

While doing post-Saudi research for this book, I interviewed a man who had worked in Yanbu on the same project I had worked on. We never met while in Saudi but had heard of each other. As we exchanged war stories, it became clear that we each loved diving and exploring archeological sites. Then, just in casual conversation, he mentioned that he and another diver had found the place where Moses crossed the Red Sea.

Now I had thought about Moses just about every time I went diving there. Everywhere I dove, though, it was the same scenario: There was a massive barrier reef, a sheer cliff, and a very steep drop-off into water that was over one thousand feet deep. Because of what I had seen, I had decided that the Bible scholars who said that Moses actually crossed a swampy area at the northwest end of the Red Sea were probably right. I was skeptical, but I listened to the man's story.

"We were diving quite a ways north of the hundred-kilometer sharm," he said. "We were following the reef north and came to an unnatural break in the reef that extended for at least four hundred meters. The area in the break had a gently sloped sand bottom that extended out into the deep water. It looked like a freeway on ramp. There was no natural reason for the break or for the lack of plant life on the sand bottom. It had to be where Moses came across."

He told me where to look should I ever go back (fat chance if this book gets published). He expressed an interest in returning someday with cameras and better diving equipment. He said they had returned several times to the site to look for chariot wheels or whatever they might find. They found nothing, but he is convinced it is the place.

Although the story is amazing, the teller is a professional man with a good reputation. After thinking about what he told me, and after thinking about what I know first hand, I believe the place he found may very well be the actual site where Moses first entered the barren wilderness. It is directly across from Egypt, and it is only a few hundred miles from what is now Israel.

Is his discovery genuine? Are there any artifacts to verify the site? If you have the means, go and see for yourself. If you follow the reef north from Yanbu, you will eventually find the Moses site. There is not much chance that it would have grown over with new coral; that would take centuries. Anyway, if you are any kind of believer, or even just an optimist, the absence of coral at that site seems to hint at divine intervention.

Even if you somehow miss the Moses onramp, you will still discover what every diver who has gone there knows: The best part of the Promised Land is underwater.

Trying to Blend

Pets Help (if you can keep the laborers from eating them)

EUPHORIC DEPRESSION

A shipwrecked Robinson Caruso found himself in a strange world. The novel tells of Caruso's difficulty in adjusting to his new environment. It tells of his adventures, his successes and his failures. At times he is euphoric, at times he is depressed, and at times he is angry. His story is timeless. It should be required reading for anyone going to Saudi Arabia.

Saudi Arabia is a strange world. The people look and smell different. The food, the housing, the transportation, the landscape and the climate are different. Politics are different; the laws are different. Living there is a nonstop series of physical and psychological adjustments.

The physical adjustment consists of getting over jet lag (one week), getting over the effects of the required immunization shots (one week to ten days), and then allowing the intestines to repopulate with the local bacteria (one year or more). During the physical adjustment period, diarrhea and flu-like symptoms will come and go as the body makes the necessary adjustments. Barring an outbreak of Ebola, or a bite from a Malaria-infected mosquito, the physical adjustment is uncomfortable but not terribly eventful. The psychological adjustment, on the other hand, can be quite eventful.

The psychological process known as "culture shock" can be divided into four phases. The first phase begins when the plane lands. A person is so overwhelmed with new information that they become euphoric. Newcomers walk around in a wide-eyed, mouth-open state of amazement. Everything is wonderful. Everything is beautiful, and everything is so exciting. If their spouse is with them, their sex life improves. If they are alone, not enough time has passed to be concerned about sex.

Occasionally, a newcomer will be so shocked by what he sees and smells that he demands to be sent home on the next flight out. Of course, being under contract, he is not allowed to leave unless he has a prearranged escape clause or he has a bona fide medical emergency that cannot be treated locally.

The second phase sets in as the first phase winds down. A person starts to see the garbage, the chaos, the social problems and the political oppression. During the transition between the first and second phase, a person is likely to move back and forth between justifying the cultural differences and condemning them. Once a person sees how alien this new world actually is, he enters the second phase of adjustment—chronic depression.

The second phase, depending on the individual, will last from three months to several years. Some individuals never escape from this phase. Some individuals lose their appetite and lose weight. Most eat for comfort and become overweight. People going through this phase do not realize how depressed they are until after they are clear of the malady. It is common for a person to reflect back and say, "Man, was I ever depressed back then."

During the second phase, a person can often function at work OK as long as the job doesn't require a smile or cheerful attitude. Many workers suffering through this phase do what is required of them but have below-normal performance. It is during this phase that many individuals have work-related injuries or traffic accidents. A few commit suicide.

This phase gradually gives way to the third phase— frustrated anger. In this phase, the person is still depressed but will no longer accept the condition. They become frustrated and angry. They may become antisocial. People in this phase lash out at their friends about the problems they see around them. Some individuals become quite rude to the local population. It is in this phase that a person is most likely to learn of the Arab word "calaboose" (jail). Some people in this phase refer to the local population with slurs such as "rag-heads" or "sand-niggers." These same people, once past the angry phase, often become avid pro-Arab supporters who would be repulsed by such language. Then again, some people are just bigots. For die-hard bigots, there are only three phases to their adjustment.

If a person has the will to shake off the ethnocentric shackles, it is possible to make it to the fourth phase. In the fourth phase, a person accepts the culture as normal. In effect, he becomes part of the culture—he feels at home. In this final phase, a person may develop such cultural relativism that his or her identity is totally entwined with the local culture. A person who has reached this level of adjustment has adopted many of the local mores and values and may have difficulty reentering his native culture. Such a person may experience all four phases of adjustment upon reentering his homeland.

Although the cultural-shock phenomenon occurs upon moving to any new culture, there is one phenomenon that is unique to Saudi Arabia. I have talked to many other expatriates who have each experienced the same thing. Upon leaving the country, there is an involuntary letdown reflex that happens as soon as the plane leaves the runway. The body relaxes completely. It feels as if every muscle in your body is simultaneously and involuntarily relaxing. It is a great feeling.

Everyone I talked to about this phenomenon has drawn the same conclusion. The letdown is the release of the chronic stress that every expatriate in Saudi Arabia must endure. The chronic stress is caused by chronic endangerment. Even for those who have made it to the fourth phase of adjustment, the Saudi stress syndrome is unavoidable. The universal sentiment is, "Lord, it feels good to leave that place."

After spending most of a nine-year-period in the Middle East, I called it quits and returned to the United States. Saudi Arabia and Kuwait had become too comfortable. In my heart of hearts, I was becoming an Arab. If I had not left when I did, I would have stayed until I retired or died. Though I knew I had to go home, I was more apprehensive of going back to the United States than I had been of going to the Middle East. My gut just told me that things would not be the same.

The first day back, I went to a local grocery store to buy a few things. Upon entering the line for the checkout, I found that the woman in front of me was wearing a bikini. She wore it well. I just flat didn't know what to do. I sort of expected a Mutawwi'un to swoop down and arrest her. In my mind, I visualized an angry crowd outside the store, stones in hand, just waiting for the prostitute to step outside. She turned and smiled. I stood their frozen with my mouth open. It would have been appropriate to say "hello." I just gawked. The adjustment process was beginning.

So much had changed in nine years. I had missed nine years of movies and TV. People would say things about actors, or the characters they played, and I didn't have a clue as to whom they were talking about. When I admitted to one guy that I had never heard of the TV show he was going on and on about, he quipped, "What planet did you come from?" I explained my situation, which he found amusing. It wasn't all that funny to me. I felt like a relic from a time capsule. The movies and shows I knew about were long forgotten. Thank God for *Star Trek*. It was my only link to this new culture.

The subtle differences really frustrated me. On my first trip to an ARCO AM/PM gas station, I became angry because I couldn't get the pump to work. When I went inside to complain, I found that I had to pay first. Inwardly, I wondered what kind of new crap was this? I paid and pumped. When I came in for my change, I asked for a Coke. The clerk pointed out the soda machine.

"I get it myself?" I asked in shock.

"Yah, its right over there," she shot back.

After filling my soda, I went to the counter to pay. "Can I have a straw?"

"What, you didn't see the straws next to the soda machine?"

If I had a tail, it would have been between my legs as I went back and got a straw. I walked back to the register to thank her and to apologize for my ignorance. She nervously acknowledged my apology and then kept staring at me as I walked out. The staring really puzzled me. I wondered if my unfamiliarity with current American culture stood out so much that everyone would stare at me until I learned to blend. It bothered me so much that I mentioned it to my wife who was holding the door open for me.

As we drove away, my wife told me that I shouldn't worry about being odd. She said I really didn't stand out that much as long as I kept my mouth shut. She then told me the real reason for the clerk's stare.

"When you went back to get your straw, the girl asked me what your problem was. I told her to cut you a little slack because you had been in prison for a long time and had not yet mastered the outside world."

I wanted to go back to clear my name, but my wife convinced me that it would be easier to convince the clerk that I had been abducted by aliens. In a sense, that was closer to the truth. It's a shame no one ever wrote about what happened to Robinson Caruso when he returned home. I would have found such a book quite useful.

Christopher A. Larsen

Exploring the Bones of A Woody

Discovering Yanbu Al Nahkal With The Family

Jogging Down a Sand Dune

WHY GO?

People go to run away. People go to get rich. People go because their company transferred them, or because they didn't know what they were getting into. One old German man, an ex-Nazi, told me he went because there were no Jews in Saudi Arabia (he seriously underestimated the Mosad). The real reason people go, though, is the same as it has been since Columbus set sail—for adventure.

Moving to the Middle East is not unlike moving to another state. Even a domestic move requires a certain amount of adventure. There are new streets, new stores, new scenery, new friends and a new job. Dealing with all the changes is an adventure. The whole experience is a combination of disasters and delights. Moving to the Middle East is like that, just more intense.

The intensity of the adventure is driven by the forbidden and the strange, and everything in the Middle East is forbidden and strange. Some innocent acts that are acceptable in our world are considered criminal in the Middle East. Learning the taboos is part of the adventure. Surviving the infractions is a game. Staying out of jail is the goal. If all goes well, you end up with some great stories and some great slides. If all goes poorly, you end up as an action item on the American Ambassador's daily planner.

Some adventures are fairly safe. The standard safe adventure is a visit to the local suik. Everything legal is sold at the suik. These primitive malls are usually located near the center of each town. They are an open-air affair with some stalls covered and some not. The odors drifting through the suik vary from delightful near the coffee and spice market to quite disgusting near the meat market. The sights also vary—quite delightful near the carpet and the gold market—quite disgusting near the meat market.

The first time I ventured into an old suik, I was transported back a thousand years in time. Strolling through that ancient market place, I daydreamed of running into Ali Baba or Sinbad at the next turn. There were many voices but few recognized words. Everyone dressed funny. Men wore white and women wore black. Everyone except me wore sandals. Some passed by with the aroma of several days worth of heavy perspiration. Others passed by reeking of strong perfume. Women with packages carried them on top of their heads or in large woven bags with shoulder straps. Men with packages either had their women carry them or they had a donkey carry them. The moving crowd would occasionally part making way for a donkey pulling an old wooden cart retrofitted with modern rubber tires mounted on fifteen-inch Chevy rims.

For me, the donkey carts with Chevy wheels broke the spell. There was just enough twentieth-century garbage visible to remind me where I really was. With a squint of the eyes, though, and a little imagination, it was still the year 977 and I was living one of those *1001 Arabian Nights* stories. One tall, thin Arab passed by with one of those curved daggers on his hip. Was his name Ali? Could his family name have been Baba?

On that first visit to the suik, one particular piece of merchandise caught my eye. It was probably a manifestation of my daydream. I spotted one of those old curved knives that was just so Arabian-Knightish. I had to buy it for my dad. I paid way too much (twice the USA Price), but it was a valuable experience.

The knife purchase was a lesson on how not to buy things in the Middle East. I saw the knife. I liked the knife. I enthusiastically asked, "How much?" I paid the asking price and walked away happy. When I told my friend who had brought me to the suik what I had paid, he laughed and explained to me how every aspect of what I had just done was wrong.

He explained how you must develop an attitude before you arrive at the suik. You must set in your mind that you don't want, don't need, and don't have any use for what is being sold.

You must have it set in your mind that to make a purchase is to do the vendor a favor—and you don't owe him a favor. You must be committed to paying no more than 50% of the asking price. If you don't have the skills to haggle the price down to at least half the asking price, don't buy. Then, you must learn the most appropriate negotiating method for your personality. If you are aggressive and angry, be more aggressive and angry. If you are timid and meek, learn to say "thank you" and quickly turn to walk away (a good vendor won't let you actually leave). Whatever trick gives you the edge, learn it well. Just remember, if you pay half the asking price for whatever you buy, the value of your take-home pay is effectively doubled.

On my second visit to the suik, I had another experience that taught me a valuable lesson about being aware of the world around me and about minding my own business. Actually, I had just left the suik and was walking back to my car. I was parked a few blocks away from the suik. It wasn't a parking lot per say; it was just an area where everyone parked. As I passed by a cluster of five or six Mercedes cargo trucks, I noticed a group of Bedouin drivers sitting on several carpets they had placed on the ground between their trucks. Curious, I walked closer and noticed that they were playing cards. I noticed a pile of currency on the carpet. I also noticed that the trucks kind of formed a wall between the players and the rest of the world. I figured they parked their trucks that way to block the wind. In my euphoric condition, I didn't stop to consider where I was or what I was actually observing. I raised my camera and said, "Hey, do you guys mind if I take your picture?"

I doubt they understood my words. They did, however, understand that I was pointing a camera at their illegal gambling activity. The whole group simultaneously jumped up and came after me. I was young then and had running shoes. They were old and had sandals. I outran them and hid behind some other trucks. They went back to their trucks and each drove away. When I was sure it was safe, I walked to my car and drove home. I worried for awhile that one of the drivers would track me down and demand the photos and negatives that I didn't have time to take. That incident gave me the resolve to learn more about my new world. It also provided me with a whole series of important insights that allowed me to survive my nine-year adventure: Keep your mouth shut; observe from a distance; if spotted, avert your eyes; be aware of the world around you and always wear running shoes.

Although many Middle East adventures are just strange fun, some can be dangerous and life threatening. A friend, who does not want to be named, told me of his adventures near Al Karj (an agricultural area near Riyadh). While driving in a rural area, he was nearly run off the road by a speeding Mercedes. A few miles down the road, he spotted the same Mercedes stopped beside the road (a nature call or something like that). He was still agitated and decided to stop and vent his anger. He pulled in behind the Mercedes and got out just as the driver was coming out of a grove of date palms. He started yelling at the driver. The driver calmly walked up to my friend and shoved a 9mm pistol up under my friend's jaw.

"Are you suggesting that I do not know how to drive?" the man calmly asked with no accent.

"Well, no. I just had a bad day and was foolishly shooting my mouth off. I don't want any trouble. Please forgive my rude behavior," was the best my rattled friend could muster.

The obviously well educated Saudi smiled and said "Go now, before I decide to take personally your rude behavior."

My friend immediately took the man's advice. In retrospect, my friend guessed the man to be either some low-level prince (it was only a Mercedes) or the man was a member of the Saudi Secret Police. Either way, my friend decided to continue his adventuring with a bit more caution.

Another friend told me of a Friday-morning trip he made to a rural town near Riyadh. He parked his truck and was walking toward the suik when he noticed a crowd of Saudis gathered near a mosque. He cautiously walked closer, trying to appear as if he was just walking by. He stopped, though, when he saw why everyone had gathered together. There was a Saudi woman buried up to her waist in the sand. There was a pile of rocks off to one side. After a few more words from the Mutawwi'un who was obviously sponsoring the event, the crowd moved to the pile of stones. Each person picked up as many rocks as possible and began throwing them at the woman. After the crowd had pelted her with several hundred rocks, the woman was dazed and bleeding but not dead. The Mutawwi'un motioned for everyone to move aside. With the wave of the Mutawwi'un's arm, a Mercedes dump truck, fully loaded with large skull-sized rocks, backed up to the where the woman was and dumped the entire load on top of her.

At that point, my friend continued walking. He couldn't help looking back, though. The Mutawwi'un caught his glance. My friend said, "You know, that's the only time I have ever seen a Mutawwi'un smile."

Although I never personally witnessed an execution, I did have a few exciting moments of my own. On one photographic expedition with my wife, we came across a Bedouin family traveling through the desert with camels, goats and one Toyota pickup. We were so fascinated with the scene that we stopped our truck and started shooting pictures. We were vaguely aware that the Toyota truck had zoomed off behind a hill. As we continued to shoot I heard the Toyota come up on my left side (we were shooting on the right side of our truck). I heard the Toyota door slam and turned toward the sound just as the Bedouin's arm came through my open window. He grabbed my camera and wrenched it from my hand. If the strap had not been around my neck, he would have made off with it. As it was, I was barely able to catch it on the way out the window. Being twice his size allowed me to wrench it back.

With my limited Arabic vocabulary, I was able to discern from his shouting and gesturing that he was upset because we had taken photos of his wife. When it was understood that he was not going to get my camera, the man wanted feluce (money). Instead of giving him money, I took the exposed film from my camera and handed it to him. He took it, insulted me one more time and went back to his truck. Looking back, I wish I had given him money. Those were some great shots.

A month or so after the picture-taking incident, my wife's visa ran out. She was too pregnant to leave the country for another visa, so she stayed illegally until after our son was born. Driving around the country with an expired visa is an adventure in itself. Knowing that we both risked jail, a fine, and deportation just made it more exciting. We dodged checkpoints on a regular basis. Watching out for anyone that might be checking papers made us so aware of what was going on around us that we took in every detail. Our heightened awareness allowed us to see things we would have otherwise overlooked.

On one trip into Yanbu, the closest town to our camp, we found ourselves in a serious traffic jam. We were on a six-lane road with a concrete divider in the middle. We were in the inside lane next to the concrete divider. What we thought was a traffic jam turned out to be makeshift checkpoint. By the time we realized what was going on, we were only three cars away from the police. In my mind, I heard the sharp clang of the jail door closing.

As we pondered our inevitable arrest, the car in front, and the two cars to his right, moved forward. The two cars to my right did not move (they were fumbling with their papers). I jammed on the gas and cut between the stopped cars on my right and those that had just moved forward. Without thinking it through, I headed off-road into the desert. As I accelerated away from the town, I looked in my mirror and saw a cloud of dust behind me that most certainly had to be the police. As the dust-cloud fell back, my confidence rose. Unfortunately, the hill in front of me was rising faster than my confidence. As I veered left to take an oblique angle to the hill, I noticed that the vehicles behind me were also veering left and were running parallel to us. The sweat was building-up on my forehead when my wife began shouting: "Slow down, slow down; those cars behind us are not the police. Those are the same two cars that were stopped just to the right of us back at the checkpoint."

Well, we weren't arrested. We didn't go to jail. We weren't even really chased—but it was a genuine heart-throbbing adventure nonetheless. Over the next few years, we had many such near-serious adventures. One or two angels were always there when needed. We, of course, kept them always in demand.

Most of the trouble we almost got ourselves into was not really our fault. We sometimes went into the desert on weekends to camp. Sometimes we would run into other people or animals, sometime not. On one occasion, while living in Kuwait, we decided to go north of the city toward the hills that were visible in the distance. Since the hills were the only visibly different landscape in any direction, they were naturally quite appealing to a pair of adventurous campers. We did not realize that the hills were smack on the Iraqi border. (This was three years before the Gulf War when the USA was helping the Iraqis and the Iranians fight each other.)

As we drove away from the city toward the hills, we did notice that we were the only vehicle on the road. As the city shrank in our rear view mirror, we also noticed a sign now and then, but they were all in Arabic. Then, just as we were close enough to really become interested in the hills looming five or six clicks away, we saw a sign written in Arabic, English and a few other languages.

I still remember the exact wording: "Unauthorized personnel traveling beyond this point will be shot!" We did not cross even the crack in the road. We stopped, backed up, then turned around. We found a less interesting place to camp south of town.

Some of my best adventures, though, were not life threatening. Some adventures were as simple as attending a Saudi wedding celebration and having to share a meal of roasted sheep, rice and fruits. The food was good, but two things made the evening particularly difficult for me—the roasted sheep still had its head and eyeballs—and I am left handed.

It's a problem being left-handed in the Middle East. Saudis don't use toilet paper; they use their left hand. Of course, they do wash their hand afterwards, but it is still a serious breach of etiquette to eat with your left hand. Saudis do not use silverware. If you touch the food with your left hand, they throw both you and the food out the back door.

Even if a person is naturally right handed, it is still difficult for a novice to eat at such a feast. Anyone can grab a hand-full of food, but getting it into your mouth without touching your mouth with your hand is quite a trick. The Arabs grab small amounts of food and then throw the food into their open mouth. It looks easy enough, but just try it right-handed when you are a left-handed person. After a few complete misses and a few grains of rice up my nostrils, an observant host (with a knowing smile) handed me a paper plate and plastic fork. Holding my left hand completely under the plate, I took some food and retreated to a nearby table. Just to be safe, I kept my left hand tucked in my belt behind my back.

During the nine-year period that I worked in the Middle East, I had many small adventures and a few large ones. When not off adventuring, I was sharing my adventure stories with other expatriates. Often times, we would swap stories long into the evening. In a sense, we were like warriors, reworking our bumbling adventures into moments of conquest and victory. It was as much fun hearing the next guy's story as it was reliving my own.

One old guy, an ex-Nazi who had hid-out much of his adult life in a South-American jungle, told of his encounters with Jaguars, poisonous snakes, Caymans, headhunters, insects and diseases. To listen to him talk, you would think that Indiana Jones was a boy scout.

"You know," he said, "all those things happened to me, but they didn't all happen at once. The jungle was so beautiful, but much of the time it was monotonous and it was a great internal struggle just to survive another day. Looking back, it was one large adventure composed of many small pieces. But you know, the time spent between those many small pieces was for me a prison sentence."

Like the old German, we each had our own tragic personal stories. Most of us were running from something. We each took our small pills of adventure with large gulps of depression and loneliness. Although our stories were each quite different, we all had one common bond—an intense need for adventure. I have no doubt that had we all been born five hundred years earlier, the lot of us would have been swapping adventure stories on the deck of the Santa Maria.

Christopher A. Larsen

At The End of The Day, There is Always TV (roof next door)

RIFAT

In 1980, I believed all Palestinians were terrorists. I didn't actually know any Palestinians; I just knew what I had heard through the media. There was always a bus being blown up or a suicide bomber in a restaurant. Whoever those Palestinians were, they certainly didn't share our value for life. It was with that prejudice that I met Rifat Lubani, a card-carrying member of the PLO.

Rifat, a civil engineer, managed a large general contracting company in Yanbu, Saudi Arabia. I managed a project that was subcontracted from his company. During our first meeting, Rifat offered me a cup of Lipton® tea with a little too much sugar and way too much condensed milk. He wanted to know my weaknesses, and I wanted to know about Palestinians. After the required polite exchanges, I told him, "I understand that you Palestinians are all terrorists."

"Terrorists!" he shouted. "You think we are terrorists? If you want to know about terrorists, I will tell you about the father of all terrorism, Menachem Begin."

As he told me how Menachem Begin started terrorism in the Middle East, I wondered how much of his story was memory and how much was politically implanted. In 1980, I had no way to confirm his story, and Arabs can be so dramatic. His quivering voice brought tears to my eyes as his story unfolded.

Rifat's story begins in April of 1948 when he was in the sixth grade. He lived with his parents and grandparents on a small farm in a village near Jerusalem. He had uncles, brothers and sisters, but I do not remember how many. I do remember, though, that he had fewer at the end of the story than at the beginning.

On 9 April 1948, Menachem Begin, then a young officer, led a raid on Rifat's village. When Begin's commandos entered the schoolyard, Rifat and several other children ran and hid. Rifat hid behind a wall as many of his slower classmates were gunned down by machine-gun fire. As he ran home, he saw one commando bayonet a pregnant woman in the belly as she ran across a street. The soldiers went through the village indiscriminately throwing hand grenades into homes—American-made hand grenades.

The soldiers poured gasoline into the village granary and burned it. They just shot people at random. Some they let pass; some they did not. In a matter of hours, several hundred people were dead—mostly the young. Out of fear that the commandos would return, the survivors abandoned their homes and walked to Lebanon. Rifat swears that the next morning before everyone left they pulled more than one hundred and fifty bodies of children from the communal well—most of them under the age of twelve.

Rifat's grandfather tried to go back to their farm to find some of their livestock but was stopped a few hundred yards from the village. His grandfather told him that the young soldier spoke Arabic saying, "Go on old man; get out of here. I don't want to waste a bullet on you." His grandfather took the advice and caught up with the family.

Rifat, and what was left of his family, made it to Lebanon. There were no camps when they arrived. Those where built later. The first days in Lebanon were spent in chaos and on the ground. They arrived with only the clothes on their back, a few blankets and precious little food. Some family members who escaped the village did not survive the first few months in exile.

Rifat grew up as a refugee in Southern Lebanon. His remaining family worked hard to put him through college. He earned his engineering degree at the American University of Beirut. He was bitter about what had happened to his family, but he did not hate all Jews. He told me that a few of his old neighbors were Jewish and that two of them were killed in the raid. Rifat believes the problem in his homeland was not caused by native Jews. The problem was caused by the Zionistic zeal brought in by Jews who emigrated from Europe after World War II. "Those Jews," he said, "were filled with righteous hatred."

He knew that the Holocaust was the seed for their hatred; he just didn't appreciate being the fertilizer. He was also very critical of the United States and Great Britain for their role in stealing his homeland.

He said, "If someone came and killed part of your family, and you were forced to leave your home and your country, how would you feel about those people? What would you do?" He paused for a while and studied my face, then asked, "How can your government support a group of people that would slaughter our families and steal our land?"

"No problem," I told him. "It's an American tradition. How do you think we got our land? Do you really expect the U.S. Government to view Palestinians any differently than it did Native Americans?"

My cynicism toward my own government was taken by Rifat as callousness. Our conversation was a bit awkward after that. Perhaps I should have told him that my grandfather, for whom I was named, lived with Native Americans in Wyoming until he was nearly thirty-five. I could have explained how much my own grandfather hated the U.S. Cavalry. Then again, it's probably better that I didn't. I would have added something like, "You know, the Jews think their story of oppression is unique, too." That would have really ticked him off. Anyway, after that first meeting, Rifat concluded that I was just another crude American who didn't share his value for life. With that enlightenment, we became more or less friends.

Rifat's story was moving, but it was just his story. Over the years, I have tried to collaborate his story by talking to other Palestinians and to a few Israeli Jews. The Palestinians claimed it all happened as Rifat said. The Israeli Jews had either never heard about it or claimed it was a Palestinian lie, but then, some Germans claim the Holocaust was a Jewish lie. Eight hours of research on the Web, though, yielded enough Israeli war stories to fill several volumes. One story matched fairly closely with Rifat's story; it was about a massacre in the village of Deir Yassin. I found firsthand accounts and photographs taken by

Palestinians. I also found a website of denial put up by one Jewish individual. For a good overview of what I found, go to www.deiryassin.org.

I have decided that Rifat is not a terrorist. He is just a man, no better and no worse than the rest of us. He dreams of restoring Palestine, but that dream is no more realistic than Golda Meir's unrealized goal of expanding Israel's borders from the Nile to the Tigris Euphrates. (That would have been all of the Middle East.)

To be fair, some Palestinians are terrorists, but then so are some Irish, some Japanese and some Americans. Such madness has no respect for the boundaries of culture, religion or time. It is the twisted logic justifying the Holocaust. It is a voice from God telling Yigal Amir to assassinate Yitzhak Rabin. It is the passionate hatred behind ethnic cleansing. It is a dark sickness in man's heart, a plague on man's soul. No one is immune, not even Jewish war heroes. Blinded by ethnic superiority, Begin's commandos overlooked a simple truth—the death of one's child is no less devastating to a Palestinian.

Over the past decade, the U. S. Government has invested a lot of tax dollars toward brokering peace in the Middle East. As volatile as politics in Israel have proven to be, though, I fear these efforts may be causing as many problems as they are solving. (Remember Somalia?) Life in Israel is too complex for U.S. Bureaucrats to understand. The only one who can really help the Arabs and Jews get along is God, and as Rifat lamented, "We can't even agree on what to call Him."

ABOUT THE AUTHOR

Christopher Larsen was born in Omaha, Nebraska in 1948. He served in the U.S. Navy during the Viet Nam War. He earned a B.S. in Business Administration from the University of Phoenix. He lived in Saudi Arabia from 1977 through 1985. He also lived one year in Kuwait. He now resides in Las Vegas, Nevada where he works as a water management consultant.

When Chris returned to live in the United States, he found a different world than the one he had left. He had missed nine years of movies and TV. The music was different and attitudes were different. The thing that bothered him the most, though, was the negative attitude that most people had toward Arabs. It bothered him so much that he started writing stories to show Arabs as the people they really are: some good, some bad, and some ordinary. Those stories led to other stories about the expatriate experience. The best of these stories are in this book.

www.ingramcontent.com/pod-product-compliance
Lightning Source LLC
Chambersburg PA
CBHW020440290526
45785CB00002B/941